FAMILIES THAT
PLAY
TOGETHER
STAY
TOGETHER!

Bethany House Books
by Donna Partow

Becoming a Vessel God Can Use
Families That Play Together Stay Together
(with Cameron Partow)
How to Work With the One You Love (with Cameron Partow)
No More Lone Ranger Moms

9610

FAMILIES THAT PLAY TOGETHER STAY TOGETHER!

CAMERON & DONNA PARTOW

BETHANY HOUSE PUBLISHERS
MINNEAPOLIS, MINNESOTA 55438

Published by Bethany House Publishers
A Ministry of Bethany Fellowship, Inc.
11300 Hampshire Avenue South
Minneapolis, Minnesota 55438

Printed in the United States of America.

Library of Congress Cataloging-in-Publication Data

Partow, Cameron.
    Families that play together stay together: fun and healthy TV-free ideas /
Cameron and Donna Partow.
      p. cm.
    ISBN 1-55661-711-9
     1. Family recreation. 2. Physical fitness. 3. Games. 4. Travel.
I. Partow, Donna. II. Title.
GV182.8.P295   1996
790.1'91—dc20   96-35651
                                                          CIP

Special Thanks To:

Our girls, Nikki, Leah, and Taranee. Thanks for behaving yourselves while we worked to complete this book!

Diane Lilly, who came to the rescue during the final hours . . . as usual.

Gary and Mary Ann Reichard, for being "roll-up-the-shirt-sleeves" kind of friends. Thanks for coming through, time and again.

Phil and Beverley Phillips, for kindness and generosity above and beyond what's reasonable. We really miss you guys.

Ann Meo, Gayle Laberrare, Nancy Martineau, Olga Power, Kelly Sampson, Susie Sennewald, Helen Stellwag, and Cathy Swope, a.k.a. the "Hey, there's a baby on the way!" committee. Thanks for lending a hand when Donna went down for the count.

Extra special thanks to our wonderful hosts, who graciously accommodated our active family during the final weeks of writing this book. We appreciated the opportunity to conduct final "field-testing" of our ideas:

Hotel del Coronado
Tanque Verde Ranch
The Wickenburg Inn

And our heavenly Father, who continues to shower us with blessings and the strength to be . . . "an active family."

In addition to leading an active family lifestyle, Cameron and Donna Partow work together in their speaking and writing ministry. They are co-authors of *How to Work With the One You Love* (Bethany House, 1995). Donna has also written *Homemade Business* (Focus on the Family, 1992), *No More Lone Ranger Moms* (Bethany House, 1995), and *Becoming a Vessel God Can Use* (Bethany House, 1996). Their active family includes a teenager, a six-year-old, and a brand-new baby.

The Partows offer a fun and inspiring, full-day seminar based on "Play Together, Stay Together," which they'd be glad to present to your church or community group. (Shorter presentations also available.) If your church sponsors an annual women's retreat, perhaps they would be interested in learning more about Donna's special weekend program on "Becoming a Vessel God Can Use." She is also available for luncheons and one-day events. For more information, contact:

Partow Communications
3764 N. Sawtooth Circle
Mesa, AZ 85215
(602) 807–3882
DonnaParto@aol.com

To Debbie Stafford,

who taught us that the true education of children happens in the real world, not in a classroom.

Contents

A Special Word to Fathers

I (Cameron) recently attended a Promise Keepers' gathering in San Diego, along with 50,000 other men. During the weekend, we connected via satellite with an additional 50,000 men who had gathered in Pittsburgh. It was an incredible moment when we all—100,000 strong—starting singing, "Let the Walls Fall Down."

I began thinking about the kind of walls we build. And it occurred to me that many of us men have built up walls in our own homes—walls between our children and ourselves. Walls between our wives and ourselves. I believe that nearly every man at this event has run into those walls in his own family. They have seen a need to make changes and were willing to admit they could use some practical help. They see their family members drifting apart and scattering in a thousand different directions. They see the lack of communication and growth in their relationships.

We wrote this book as a tool for all parents, but I am personally excited about the possibility of *men* taking the lead in building what we've termed an "active family lifestyle." Let me explain what I mean, one word at a time. *Active*—as opposed to sitting on the couch telling our wives (or kids) to bring us another soda. *Family*—as opposed to giving every drop of ourselves to our jobs or hobbies that keep us away from the people who need us most. And *Lifestyle*—meaning permanent, gradual change as opposed to the typical Band-Aid, quick-fix approach most of us guys prefer.

There is no denying that we are living in an age where "time" is in short supply. While at Promise Keepers, I heard a quote from Zig Ziglar that really hit home for me: "Love is spelled T-I-M-E."

There are two ways of looking at time: quantity and quality. In the 1980s, "quality time" was a buzz word among people who worked ninety hours a week but claimed that it didn't matter because when they *were* with their family, it was "quality time." Well, I have a T-shirt that reads "Quantity has a Quality all it's own." It's actually a company T-shirt, but it applies even more powerfully at home.

There's an often-quoted statistic that claims the average American father gives only twenty-seven seconds of his undivided attention to his children each day. We need to spend quantity *and* quality time with our families. We need to be with them physically *and* mentally. Unfortunately, a lot of us dads possess a special ability to be with our kids in body without really being with them at all. Notice our lack of attention while reading the paper or watching television. There in body, but not in mind.

We're not quite sure why, but we noticed that the minute our family got out of the house and broke away from the daily routine, the *quality* of our time together dramatically improved. In particular, we discovered that engaging in fun, outdoor activities broke down walls and opened lines of communication.

That's why we wrote this book. To give you practical tools you can use to build family relationships, while improving your health and creating memories that will last a lifetime. It's our hope that as you invest time to play together, your reward will be a family that stays together forever.

Part I: Fun

FAMILIES THAT PLAY TOGETHER HAVE FUN

Millions of kids can't be wrong—playing is fun! And it isn't just for the young. Introducing active play into our lives will help counter the stresses of adult life. Simple play is just fine. You don't need fancy equipment or special clothing. Playing is doing, not having.

—Gordon W. Stewart, author of *Active Living*

Chapter 1

WHY FAMILIES THAT PLAY TOGETHER STAY TOGETHER

*Since habits become power, make them work with you
and not against you.*

—E. Stanley Jones

"We should sneak out tomorrow morning," whispered our thirteen-year-old, Nikki, in a conspiratorial tone. Since teenage whispering often seems expressly designed *not for parents ears*, I was glad to be "in on" the secret for a change. We stood high atop a rugged cliff near the base of the Rincon Mountains in Tucson, Arizona. A half hour earlier, we had set out for a sunset hike with a small group of like-minded new friends at the famed Tanque Verde Ranch.*

Now we were getting the reward we'd worked for: a view to remember.

Below in the distance, nestled amid giant saguaros and acres of sagebrush, cottonwoods, and mesquite trees, was a spring-fed lake. Nearly one hundred head of cattle were spread out across the un-

---

*Tanque Verde is a 640-acre western dude ranch and four-star resort bordered by the Saguaro National Monument and the Coronado National Forest. 800–234-DUDE.

forgiving terrain; periodically, we'd hear one of them lowing plain-
tively. Our guide began explaining that since it hadn't rained in
months, the lake had become a popular watering hole—not only
for the ranch's cattle—but for deer, javelina, and even the occasional mountain lion. "Just because you want to see them, doesn't
mean they want to see you," warned naturalist Warren Fiedley.
"They'll have their fill and be gone before sunrise. The only way to
get a look is to wake up before dawn." Thus began the "conspiracy."
With a nod of my head, the plan was set.

The next morning, I was glad when baby Taranee awoke for her
five o'clock feeding, right on schedule. When she finished, I slipped
her back into the temporary crib situated in the corner of our one-
bedroom casita and crept over to the couch-bed where Nikki was
fast asleep. Within minutes we were out the door in search of adventure.

As we made our way past jagged rocks—the perfect hiding
place for rattlesnakes—I couldn't help recalling the one I'd spotted
on the trail yesterday. I was on horseback and at least ten horses
away from the critter. It was a bit unsettling, but in the kind of
adrenaline-pumping way you almost *hope* for on an adventure vacation like this. Now the thought of seeing one face-to-face (well,
face-to-foot) had me spooked. I shook it off and pressed on.

We arrived at the lake expectantly . . . but we were too late. No
deer, no dice. Disappointed but not defeated, we spotted an old
swing along the far end of the lake. Plan B was instantly set in motion. And there we sat, rocking and waiting for the sun to unleash
its full fury—the weather forecaster had called for 110 degrees. For
now, we enjoyed the fresh air and the quiet. Mostly, though, I enjoyed the contented feeling of drawing near. Of building memories
that bond, memories that bind. I enjoyed the sensation of being a
family.

Actually, *becoming* a family is more like it. Last year this time,
our little tribe consisted of Cameron, me, and five-year-old Leah.
Now here I sat, the mother of four—one in heaven and three on
earth. Reflecting on the previous year or so, I couldn't believe all

the changes we'd undergone as a family. I had lost our long-awaited second child in the fourth month of pregnancy. Then, the very week that child had been scheduled to arrive, we received a call that changed the course of our lives.

As part of the church prayer chain, I received and prayed over many requests. But the one that came in on Thursday, August 24, 1995, was different. The minute I heard the situation, I knew our family was part of the answer. Nikki, then twelve, had been left homeless after both of her parents were taken off to jail. In truth, she'd already been on her own for years, drifting from place to place. Here a week, there a month, relying on the kindness of friends . . . and strangers. Now it was official. Abandoned by her relatives, she was alone on the planet. We decided we just couldn't sleep at night in the kind of world that treats innocent children like that; we decided to take her in.

Within two weeks of her arrival, I discovered I was pregnant again. Eight months later, we had a teenager, a six-year-old, and a newborn. How on earth could we pull this family together? How could we possibly build common ground? That's the question we grappled with and you're holding (at least part of) the answer in your hands. As we have fought the forces that threatened to pull us apart, we've become convinced: families that *play together stay together.*

Advantages of the Active Family

Families who purposefully cultivate a lifestyle filled with healthy fun—who become what we've termed "an active family"—enjoy several distinct advantages over your run-of-the-mill, watch-TV-till-you-sleep, or head-in-a-thousand-different-directions American family:

- **Improved Communication.** The family that *does* together, communicates better. Think about it. How much quality communication takes place when your family is staring at the television set? Contrast that with a family gathered around a quiet campfire or watching a sunset on the beach. Now, we can't guarantee that an undistracted, peaceful environment will *make* your kids talk, but, in our experience, the chances are a whole lot better.

You see, Nikki and I weren't the only ones off on "excellent adventures" at Tanque Verde. At the end of a long day, I'd take Taranée back to the casita; that would be the cue our other girls were waiting for: Daddy time! One night, they went out in search of the illusive javelinas (never did spot one). On another, they played "jump on daddy" in the indoor pool until two o'clock in the morning. (Yes, we know that was way past bedtime, but so what? Staying up late was half the fun.)

For meals, we'd occasionally use the "divide and conquer" strategy. Mom would have an undistracted lunch with Leah, then watch the baby while Dad enjoyed one-on-one time over lunch with Nikki. It was quite a juggling act, but it was worth it because our kids *talked to us* during these special times.

- **Shared Experiences.** It's so much easier to talk with someone when you have something to talk about, isn't it? As you begin to enjoy family activities, you will build a storehouse of shared experiences you will treasure for a lifetime. Like the night the Tanque Verde Twilight Dancers taught us country line dancing, along with families from Australia, Sweden, Italy, England, and around the United States. Or the night we sang cowboy songs around the campfire.

  Together, we learned the ins-and-outs of horseback riding and had a ball watching Mom try to dismount. (Most important lesson: when you finally *do* dismount, run to the nearest hot tub. It eases sore muscles—you know, the kind of muscles you didn't know you had until they started hurting!) These are memories we'll always cherish . . . and share.

- **Common Interests.** Some of the activities you undertake in your quest to become an active family will bomb. We guarantee it! Like the time we went fishing . . . boo, hiss! Never fear, such experiences should immediately be transformed into what we call "story fodder." Even the most miserable experience is extremely valuable, because you can turn it into a hilarious story you can retell for years to come. The key is to keep exaggerating the story each time you tell it. That's what we do. The more outrageous the story becomes, the fonder the memories. We've already developed an entire comedy routine based on our ill-fated fishing trip. (But the one about our disastrous canoe trip is still the funniest. Let's put it this way: it involves capsizing and fighting for space on a low-hanging tree branch!)

Fortunately, along the way you will occasionally experience a magic moment when everyone in the family locks eyes and silently says, "Hey, this is neat." If you try enough activities, you will eventually find one that clicks with your family and becomes a common interest. *Seize it, build on it—it's a gift from God.*

- **Family Bonding and Family Identity.** Out of those shared experiences and common interests, your family will grow closer and more committed to one another. Rather than heading in a thousand different directions, like most families today, you'll be heading down the same path. Then a really exciting thing will start to happen: you will begin to develop a family identity. "We're a canoeing family." Or, "We're ski buffs." Or simply, "We're an active family." That beautiful, wonderful word "we" will ring loud and clear in the midst of a world of individualists. As a result, your family will stand out as having something extra special. And guess what? Your *kids will know it.*

- **Stress Relief.** Does your family bicker? You know, fuss and complain about nothin'? Do you take out your job and school frustrations on each other? We'll be the first to fess up: guilty, guilty, guilty on all three counts! However, we are discovering a better way to handle the stress of today's hectic world and it's medically proven to work. It's called EXERCISE, and it's what becoming an active family is all about. There is nothing on earth quite like *moving your body* to dissipate stress and get that pent-up frustration flowing in a positive direction. (Well, prayer helps, too!) As your family commits to a more active lifestyle, you will be amazed at the reduction in bickering in your home. That's a promise from our house to yours!

- **Anytime "Mini-Vacations."** Do you know families who look forward to their annual vacation all year long and then spend the whole time fighting . . . or at least fighting the inevitable disappointment? Maybe you *are* just such a family. (Yep, the Partows are guilty of that one, too!) The truth is, there's not a week on the planet that can compensate for a year of passivity and pent-up stress. (What makes a family believe that a week in an amusement park will actually *help*, is beyond us!)

  The great thing about becoming an active family is that virtually any weekend has the potential to become a mini-vacation. Think about it. A vacation is simply breaking away from the daily routine. It's getting your mind off work or the demands of caring for a home. Wouldn't a hike through the forest accomplish those objectives? Wouldn't a picnic in the country help rejuvenate you? Wouldn't climbing a challenging mountain give you a fresh perspective on the other challenges you face? The answer to all these and more is *yes*. Your active family mini-vacations will make you more productive and positive as you face your daily round of activities—including the daily job of being Mom and Dad, Sister and Brother.

  Good health and the potential for a long and happy life are the greatest gifts we can give our children. And becoming an active family is the price you pay for that gift. Don't you think it's worth it? Just to make the gift more appealing, you get some "free bonuses" with your purchase. Like the bonus of open communication, shared experiences, family bonding, family identity, and the opportunity to take mini-vacations virtually every weekend of the year. Now, aren't you excited about becoming an active family? Then you've come to the right place!

Families That Play Together Stay Together is packed with ideas and suggestions designed to help you enjoy a fun, active, family-oriented lifestyle. It even deals with the obstacles, like a teenager who is too old, too busy, too bored, and too cool to play with her family. Like a six-year-old who can't (or just plain won't) keep up. Like a newborn baby, who just wants to be held and fed and loved and has no idea she's been born into an "active family." Like a dad who is so exhausted he would rather plop down on the couch and watch TV. Like a workaholic mom who's constantly glued to her computer screen, recording "brilliant ideas" for posterity or surfing the Internet. But enough about our family!

We know from personal experience that building an active family lifestyle is easier said than done. Nevertheless, "more and more people are recognizing that physical activity and outdoor recreation—done as a family—are good not only for physical health, but for emotional health," says Susan Henley, executive director of the American Hiking Society. Pursuing that physical and emotional health *as a family* is, thankfully, a growing trend. For example, Henley now handles some five thousand inquiries a year—compared with one thousand only four years ago. "A lot of them," she reports, "are from people wanting to know which areas are suitable for families."*

Before we go any further, we want you to know that this isn't just another *celebrity fitness book*. First of all, we're not celebrities. Second, we understand that *you have a life to live*. You have a job. You have responsibilities and demands on your time. You *don't* have a private chef or a personal trainer. You *don't* have unlimited time,

*"Playing Together," by Hank Herman, *Ladies' Home Journal* (June 1991), p. 82.

energy, and resources to devote to building an active family lifestyle.

We understand. We're an ordinary family just like yours. I am far too klutzy for aerobics and would rather die than be seen wearing spandex in public. Ever since I hit thirty, I've been hovering around fifteen pounds over my ideal weight. Oh, well, I must be normal. I am far from the body beautiful, but I try to stay fit by encouraging my family to keep active. We walk, we hike, we ride bikes. We don't look great, but we sure feel good. And if *we* can do it, anyone can.

Throughout *Families That Play Together Stay Together*, you'll find charts, graphs, self-tests, personal application worksheets, and real-world homework. Although you can work through this book as an individual, we encourage you to use it *as a family*. To make it easier, we specifically designed it for use around the dinner table. Each chapter concludes with questions for discussion and suggested family activities. There's also space for a family journal, so you can record the memories and lessons you learn on your journey to a more active lifestyle.

Who knows? You may just discover that, rather than dashing in five different directions after dinner, your family may linger around the table to continue the discussion. Or better yet, you might just dash off together *in the same direction* to do something active together. Can you imagine it? It can happen!

Implementing the ideas in this book won't make you perfect. It won't make your spouse or your children perfect, either. (Hope that doesn't disappoint you!) It *will* bring your family closer together and, if you persist in an active lifestyle, it will almost certainly prolong your life and the life of your children. And it will *definitely* improve the quality of your life. If those sound like worthwhile goals to you, turn the page and let's get started. You are about to become AN ACTIVE FAMILY.

> *Say to him: "Long life to you! Good health to you and your household! And good health to all that is yours!"*
> —1 Samuel 25:6

Discussion Questions

1. Discuss each of the benefits of an active lifestyle. Let each person say which they consider to be the most important benefit and why.

2. Rate your family's activity level on a scale of 1 to 10, with 10 being the most active. Have each member discuss why he chose the rating he did.

3. Make a list of all the active things you currently do (or have recently done) *as a family*. Let each member discuss what they like/dislike about each activity.

4. Describe the most fun or exciting active thing you have ever done together. What were some lessons you learned from that experience?

5. Do you feel your family heads off in too many different directions? If you have teenagers, invite their input on the concept of heading in *the same direction* for a change. Let them voice their concerns and interests.

6. Go around the table and invite everyone to throw out ideas for active things they would like to do. Write down every idea from bungee jumping to a bonfire. This is not the time to critique! It's time to brainstorm and promote discussion.

7. Discuss your goals: where you hope to be as a family in three months, three years, three decades—and how "playing together" can help you get there.

Suggested Family Activities

1. Memorize this week's verse (1 Samuel 25:6).

2. Take a leisurely walk after dinner every night this week.

3. Set a goal to participate in a major activity by a specific date. For example, train for and compete in a 5k run within six months. Or plan a family campout within the next two months.

4. Pick one of the ideas from the above list (Question #6) . . . and go do it NOW!

Active Family Journal

Expenditure which begins at a great rate often comes to a sudden end by bankruptcy. Begin so that you can keep on, and even rise higher.

—Charles Spurgeon

Record your family goals about becoming an active family.

_____

_____

_____

_____

_____

_____

_____

_____

_____

_____

_____

_____

_____

_____

_____

_____

_____

_____

_____

_____

_____

_____

_____

_____

_____

_____

_____

Chapter 2

ACTIVE FUN FOR ORDINARY DAYS

This habit of uselessly wasting time is the whole difficulty; it is vastly important to you, and still more so to your children, that you should break the habit. It is more important to them, because they have longer to live, and can keep out of an idle habit before they are in it, easier than they can get out after they are in.

—Abraham Lincoln

In the spirit of walk before you run, look before you leap, and all those neat little clichés, we'd like to suggest some simple ideas your family can use—starting today—to increase your level of activity. (We'll be getting to the part about bungee jumping with cannibals in Irian Jaya soon enough. . . .) If your whole family is already training for the Boston Marathon, you'll want to skip this chapter. But if you think lifting your hand from the potato chip bag to your mouth is exercise, you might just find comfort knowing "a journey of a thousand miles begins with a single step." That's why Simon Says, "take two itty, bitty baby steps" before you break out the rappelling gear.

We want to assure you that becoming an active family doesn't mean you have to fly to Vail for a ski vacation (although that sure would be nice, wouldn't it?). It doesn't mean you have to frantically undertake a dozen activities or quickly get those sedentary kids signed up for baseball, basketball, and ballet lessons. The active life-style is not *frantic*. It should all be done in a spirit of fun. In fact, if at any time during the course of working through this book you realize your family is *not* having fun, not enjoying themselves, not bonding together, then back off. Somebody's taking something too seriously.

Some of the activities at the end of this chapter require as little as five minutes, while others can last as long as you like. One of our favorite activities is ordinary walking. (We bet you thought it was rock climbing, eh?) This afternoon, Leah and I went on a butterfly hunt through the neighborhood. On this particular outing, Leah used her net, but the truth is she doesn't need it. She has become so proficient at tracking the fluttering insects, she can snatch one up in her bare hands. Earlier this morning, Leah announced that a ladybug had been sighted in our yard, *in our yard*, of all places. Incredible! She was so excited, she created a painting of her new "friend" and taped it on the wall.

On another occasion, Leah came running into the house to show us that she had found a "down" feather. Not just an ordinary feather, mind you, but a *down* feather. For those of you who don't know, Leah could inform you that birds have three distinct types of feathers and that the purpose of down is to keep them warm. That's why baby birds are so fuzzy. They don't have flying feathers, just warming feathers.

Now if all this stuff sounds really ordinary to you, that's because it *is*. It's ordinary, *but* it sure beats sitting on the couch doin' nothin' and all the while complaining about how boring life is. . . . The place to start in building your active family is with ordinary, every-day activities. For many families, just *getting out of the house* each day will represent a huge first step. That first step can lead to walk-ing around the backyard, which can lead to walking around the block, which can lead to weekend walks through a local state park, which can lead to the family joining a hiking club, which can lead to a week-long walking tour of the Colorado Rockies, which might even lead to a walking tour of Europe. The point is: make a start. Step out into your backyard and see if you can help your little ones find a ladybug or a butterfly or a down feather. Begin at the beginning.

We think it is very unfortunate that there is so much pressure to get kids involved in organized activities at ever-younger ages. In the past few months, we have had various friends ask if Leah wanted to join a swim team, a soccer team, Brownies, singing lessons, and piano lessons. (No ordinary piano lessons, these, but SUZUKI lessons. Whoa! What mother could deny her child that opportunity?) Then, of course, there are the ubiquitous dance lessons and gymnastic classes. She's been invited to participate in a girl's club, and I've been sorely tempted to enroll her in an American Girl's literary discussion/craft group that meets at a local bookstore.

These activities may be good in moderation, but they can *get the family heading in too many different directions*. It can lead to families who are not active in a positive sense, but *hyper*active. Lately, we have been reading the works of Charlotte Mason, a nineteenth-century British educator—endorsed by the Queen Mother herself—who strongly advocated the importance of what she termed "Nature Study" among children.* The concept appealed to us because it's something our whole family can enjoy together, right in our own neighborhood, to add some healthy activity to ordinary days.

At the heart of nature study is the Nature Notebook, where children record their own observations of the world around them—without regard to the *right* answer. Older children can write down what they see and/or draw pictures. Younger children simply draw, color, or paint. Our daughter's painting of the ladybug is the perfect example . . . and it was *not prompted* by us. She was just playing and having fun!

A nature notebook doesn't have to cost a fortune. It just has to

---

*Her six-volume "magnum opus" is available through Great Christian Books for $43.95. To order, call 800-775-5422.

be tough enough to withstand some wear-and-tear and the paper should be thick enough that children can create color drawings without bleeding through. Ideally, you should get artist-quality paper, so the children can use a variety of art media: paint, chalk, cut-and-paste, etc. Our friend Roseann Mihm found artist-quality sketchbooks for each of her five children at a going-out-of-business sale. She paid only $6.00 each for 12"×20" notebooks with top-quality paper that will last her children for years and years.

In their outstanding book *The Wholehearted Child* (Whole Heart Press, 817-797-2142), Clay and Sally Clarkson offer ideas you can use to incorporate Charlotte Mason's philosophy of nature study into ordinary days:

- **Take nature walks as a family.** Rather than teaching about nature, simply talk about things you and your children observe, and stimulate conversation with questions: have you noticed that some trees lose their leaves and others don't? Why do you suppose God made worms? Why do rabbits have such big ears? Have each child keep a Nature Notebook in which they can record their thoughts and impressions, draw sketches of objects found or observed in nature, and consider what they can learn about God from what they see in nature.

- **Build up a good nature library:** an assortment of child-friendly field guides, quality children's reference books, good literature about nature and animals, nature media (software, videos, audiotapes), posters, and nature magazines. Some resources worth checking out include: Audubon Pocket Guides, Peterson First Guides, *Usborne Illustrated Encyclopedia of the Natural World* and Spotter's Guides (actually, *any* Usborne book—they are awesome!), Eyewitness Books, *Reader's Digest Guide to North American Wildlife* and the Kingfisher Visual Factfinder series.

- **Have your children keep a Seasons Log,** in a nice notebook by a window that allows observation. Identify a select number of things to observe: temperatures, tree leaves, flowers, garden growth, sunrise/sunset times, location of the sun, stars in the sky. Once a month, on the first day of the month, have them make a record of changes they observe.

- **Encourage your children to start simple collections of inanimate objects in nature:** leaves, wildflowers, rocks, shells. Use the collections for lessons in observation and classification. Look for Scriptures about the collected objects, as well as about wildlife that is caught or observed. Equip your children with a good set of tools for "in the field" nature study: pocket field guides, field binoculars, compass, magnifying lens, good insect net, walking stick, small pickax, multipurpose pocketknife, notebook, collection bag. We bought Leah a net for eight dollars three years ago and it is one of the best investments we ever made. She uses it constantly for catching insects, tadpoles, and she's even caught a fish.

- **Get in the habit of getting your children to look up at night** (especially when you are in the country). The best way is flat on your back, or in tilt-back chairs. Start pointing out constellations, observe the different moon phases, look for the Milky Way, try to spot planets and other heavenly bodies, look for meteors. Any field guide to astronomy will orient you to the night sky. Check out *Exploring the Sky by Day* and *Exploring the Night Sky* both by Terrance Dickinson (Camden House Publishers). We also enjoy *The Drinking Gourd* by F. N. Monjo (Harper Collins), which is actually a book about the underground railway. The drinking gourd is another name for the Big Dipper, which was used to guide "railway" travelers to the North. This book brought to life the concept that knowing how to read the night sky is important—it can even save your life if you learn to navigate by it.

- **Plan sky-watching parties for special events** such as the annual Perseid meteor shower, a lunar eclipse, or a conjunction of planets. Our kids especially enjoyed watching the space shuttle pass overhead; we learned from the news what time it would be over our town and went out about five minutes ahead of time. Sure enough, we saw what looked like a rapidly moving star appear in the distance *exactly as scheduled*. That opened a discussion on space travel and jet propulsion—we even made new friends with others who had gathered along the side of the road to watch for the shuttle.

- **Have your children keep a Night Sky Log** to chart the changes during the different seasons of the moon (rise, set, phase), the constellations, and the planets, including unusual phenomena such as halos around the moon.
  Other books we strongly recommend include *Diary of an Edwardian Lady* and the *Handbook of Nature Study*.*

Plain Old-Fashioned Play!

As much as we love learning, sometimes we also love *not learning*. Especially as a home-schooling family, sometimes we need to just turn off our brains and flat-out *play*. There's Frisbee, badminton, horseshoes, hopscotch, and freeze tag. There's volleyball, kickball, and kill the man with the ball. It makes us really sad when we discover so many children who've forgotten how to *play*. Believe it or not, professionals have actually done research and determined that today's children know less games than previous generations. That's because they're either watching TV, playing with a video game, or participating in some organized activity. They don't have the time they need for creative or unstructured play.

---

*Originally published in 1910, available through Great Christian Books, 800-775-5422.

Well, we say *make time* for creative and unstructured play! That's why we've compiled a list of games to get your family headed in a fun direction. Don't wait for a special occasion! Why not get out of the house and try some of these ideas *today*?

Ordinary Fun

Find a ladybug
Jump rope for five minutes
Do fifty jumping jacks
Do ten push-ups
Fly a kite
Try jet-skiing
Water-skiing
Play Capture the Flag
Tug-of-war
Water balloon toss
Long-jump contest
Frisbee
Fifty-yard dash races
Scuba-diving
Square-dancing lessons
Visit an art gallery
Science museum
Take a drive through the country
Do twenty sit-ups
Easter-egg style hunt (hide crayons, etc.)
Touch your toes twenty times (without bending your knees)
Ride bikes
Skip
Play horseshoes
Badminton
Tennis
Street hockey
Ice hockey
Dodgeball
Volleyball
Tobogganing

Walk to the store
Set up your own bowling alley
Count how many times you can throw a ball back and forth
    without someone missing
See how long you can keep a beach ball in the air
Build a snowman
Hopscotch
Run through the sprinklers
Have a water-gun fight
Break out the hose and have fun!
Walk around the block (fifteen minutes or more)
Pick and identify ten different types of flowers
Pick and identify ten different types of leaves
Swim five laps
Shoot a few hoops
Draw pictures with sidewalk chalk
Paint a mural with washable paint
Play Nerf ball sports
Jump on a trampoline
Play miniature golf
Go bowling
Catch a butterfly
Start a nature notebook
Walk the dog
Play kickball
Tag
Hide-and-Seek
Mother, May I
Simon Says
Musical lawn chairs (hum the music)
Ring Around the Rosy
Green Light/Red Light
Football catch
Baseball catch
Soccer
Hula hoop
Jump in a pile of leaves

Sunbathe for five minutes
Gather a bag of pine cones
Cover pinecones with peanut butter, dip in birdseed, watch
the birds enjoy
Blow bubbles
Plant a tree
Feed bread crumbs to birds
Feed dried corn to ducks or geese
Play classical music and waltz in time
Play up-beat music and make up crazy dances
Roller skate or in-line skate
Ice skate
Climb a tree
Stargaze
Study constellations
Buy or borrow a telescope, look at the skies
Roast marshmallows
See how many bird nests you can find (in given time)
Build a nest out of twigs and grass
Press flowers
Visit a planetarium
Watch the clouds
Count the stars
Skip for five minutes
Hop on one foot for a count of 100
"Fence" with two long sticks
Make up a family "cheer," with motions
Race around the block
Host a roller derby

If you want even more ideas, check out two great books from
Bethany House Publishers (800–328–6109): *Games* compiled by
Mary Hohenstein, and *Noncompetitive Games for People of All
Ages* by Susan Butler.

*There is a time for everything, and a season for every ac-
tivity under heaven.*
—Ecclesiastes 3:1

Discussion Questions

1. Discuss the idea of nature study.

2. Discuss the activities listed. Highlight those that appeal to your family.

Suggested Family Activities

1. Memorize this week's verse (Ecclesiastes 3:1).

2. Purchase Nature Notebooks for each family member (Mom and Dad, too).

3. Go on a nature walk and record your observations.

4. Make a container labeled "Outdoor Fun" or some such title. You can make it as elaborate as you wish.

5. Copy the ideas you like onto small slips of paper or cut them out of the book. Put them in the container.

6. Pull out a slip and do whatever it says. If time permits, take out another . . . and another.

7. Repeat #5 every night for a week . . . or every night for a lifetime!

Active Family Journal

We act as though comfort and luxury were the chief requirements of life, when all we really need to make us happy is something to be enthusiastic about.

—Charles Kingsley

Record your reaction to the outdoor play activities you selected.

_____

_____

_____

_____

_____

_____

_____

_____

_____

_____

_____

_____

_____

_____

_____

_____

_____

_____

_____

_____

_____

_____

_____

_____

_____

Chapter 3

ACTIVE WEEKEND FUN

While exercise may become a part *of your life, active living is a* way of life. . . . *Active living is a way of life in which physical activity is valued and integrated into daily life.*

—Gordon W. Stewart, author of *Active Living*

Does this sound like your typical weekend? Friday night—watch TV. Saturday—clean the house, mow the lawn, grocery shop, *then* watch TV. Sunday—go to church, putter around the house, get ready to go back to work, watch TV. Ho-hum. It doesn't have to be that way. With a little advance planning, your weekends can be filled with exciting adventures or relaxing discoveries.

Your Active Family Weekend

Now, it will take some sacrifices and self-discipline. You'll have to do the laundry and the groceries and the yardwork during the week. You may even have to plan, pack, and prepare for a road trip. But the rewards will be worth it. Here are some affordable ideas worth investigating:

- **Tourist Weekend.** I lived in Philadelphia for thirty years and never did the full-tilt tourist thing. Looking back, I regret it. Of course, now that we live in beautiful, sunny Arizona, we have a constant stream of out-of-state visitors coming to enjoy the weather, um, er, to see their good old friends, the Partows. We appreciate these visits because they inspire us to play the role of tour guide and take advantage of all there is to see and do.

Wherever you live, no doubt there's a rich heritage of history and culture in your own backyard, just waiting to be explored. So take the time to discover. Be forewarned, though, not every outing will be a smashing success. We once drove three hours to a tourist attraction that looked fabulous in the brochures. When we got there, we found some run-down exhibits, a couple of overpriced gift shops, a dirty, overpriced restaurant and a silly stage show. (Mind you, it wasn't *intended* to be silly, but it certainly was!)

You're sure to have events that "bomb" as well. The secret is in keeping a positive attitude. We were very discouraged as we endured the long drive home from this disappointing event with our out-of-state visitor in tow. Her only Saturday in Arizona had apparently been "wasted," and we felt just terrible. (We've since made a policy of checking out all tourists sites personally before we take our guests.) Later that night, Cameron slipped away from the family and secretly put together an outlandish costume. When he came dancing and singing down the stairs (re-creating the show), we grabbed the video camera and recorded it for posterity. His performance lasted less than ten minutes, but we spent the rest of the evening laughing about our misadventure. Now *every* visitor wants to see Cameron's world famous dance for themselves and everyone wants the privilege of watching the "forbidden" video. (You know you are a REAL friend of the Partows when we let you watch THE video!) Each time we recount the days' events, they become more exaggerated and absurd. In short, what could have been just another miserable tourist outing has become a family legend.

If you are ready to play tourist for a weekend (even

without out-of-town guests), a great place to start is with the state or city tourist bureau. (See chapter 18 for a complete listing.) Just call for an information packet and they'll be glad to help. When the bundle of brochures arrives, gather the family around and start planning your tourist weekend. You may choose a self-guided walking tour of an historic district, stroll through the artists' square, or shop fresh fruit or fish markets. Museums, parks, outdoor concerts, and activities abound in every city, but it's up to you to take advantage of the opportunities offered. Who knows? You may like it so much, you'll decide to have lots of tourist weekends.

- **Farm Weekend.** Almost all children enjoy spending time with farm animals, but in our "civilized world" such opportunities have to be created. Sensing the demand, an increasing number of family farms are opening their doors for weekend visitors. Some are simply bed and breakfasts located on a farm, while others allow you to actively participate in farm life: milking cows, gathering eggs, and the whole shebang. Before moving to Arizona, we lived near Pennsylvania Dutch Country, which offered many such farm weekends. We're glad to report that's one opportunity we *did* seize. The first "adventure" of Leah's life was a weekend at Spahr's Farm in Lititz, Pennsylvania. We wandered the corn fields, petted the cows, played with the farmyard pets, and enjoyed the simple life for a while. We watched with fascination as nearby Amish farmers enjoyed an even simpler life. The Amish shun all modern conveniences, including electricity, modern farm equipment, and automobiles. They travel by horse-and-buggy and plow their fields with oxen. It was like visiting another world or another place in time, yet it was only a couple hours' drive from home. Leah loved it and so did Mom and Dad. The Pennsylvania Dutch Convention and Visitors Bureau offers a free guide listing farm vacations. Call 800-723-8824 (ext. 2445).

There's also a wonderful book by Pat Dickerman called *Farm, Ranch, and Country Vacations in America*. Pat has been releasing and updating this full-color guidebook for forty years. It offers a state-by-state listing of working ranches, dude ranches, farms, lodges, country inns, and bed and breakfast farms. Each detailed listing covers everything from a description of the facilities (many include wonderful photos) and the activities offered, to recommended ages and pricing. We think you'll find this a most inspiring guide. To order, call 800-252-7899 and be sure to tell Pat we sent you.

- **Old-Fashioned Weekend.** Here's the kind of project home-schoolers like us especially love, but we think any family will enjoy. Actually, this would be a fun project for several families to try together. In advance, research a period of history you would like to re-create. Find out as much as you can about how the families actually lived: everything from gathering food and fuel to cooking and cleaning. Read books and rent movies about that time period. As you can imagine, such an undertaking could take days or *weeks*, depending upon how involved you want to get. One option would be to devote an entire weekend to research.

  Once you've completed the research and assembled the necessary equipment, you're ready to go back in history for a weekend. Again, some families might want to make elaborate costumes, while others may simply choose to turn off all modern conveniences. It will be a stimulating—and very *physically demanding* weekend—as your family rediscovers a simpler life. (You may even want to look at old photographs from previous centuries, and will note how few overweight people there were. That's because daily living required so much more physical exertion than it does now. The exception, of course, were the extremely wealthy who had servants to do all the physical labor. Hence, being overweight was once considered a status symbol. It meant you were wealthy enough to live a life of leisure.)

- **Gardening Weekend.** We have a number of friends who set aside several weekends every year to devote to their garden, and it has become a great tradition for their families. There's a weekend where everyone gathers to prepare and plant the garden. (Depending upon the size of your family and the size of the garden, preparation and planting may require two separate weekends.) And another weekend when the whole family works to clear out the garden for the end of the season. Of course, there's usually one person in every family who is the official gardener, responsible for maintaining it throughout the season, and that's fine. But gardening weekends give everyone from Dad on down to the toddlers a chance to roll up their sleeves, enjoy the fresh air, and get filthy dirty for a good cause. Gardening is not only *great* exercise, it promises a harvest of healthy eating, too.

- **Backyard Camp-Out.** Most of us spend way too much time cooped up in our houses. So why not declare the house off-limits for an entire weekend? Make sure the weather plans to cooperate, and, to prevent mutiny, you might want to make the bathroom facilities the exception to the "nobody in the house" rule. Make a great adventure of it: cook, eat, sleep, and play outdoors. You don't have to haul out the suitcases, load up the car, worry about traffic or answer, "Are we there yet?" Your mini-vacation can begin as soon as you reach your own backyard. Pitch a tent, build a "campfire" grill or hibachi for roasting marshmallows, sing campfire songs, tell stories, and identify constellations. If the tenting life lights a fire in your family's heart, you can graduate to a real live camping trip.

- **Marathon Weekend.** Here's how to get active for a good cause: join an "a-thon." Could be a Walk-a-thon (Contact National Multiple Sclerosis Society at 800-FIGHT-MS or The March of Dimes at 800–525-WALK); a Bike-a-thon (Coast to Coast Bicycle Classic, 800–433–0528) or a Run-a-thon (Race for the Cure, 800–462-9273). We've participated in several and have found it very satisfying. By the way, the reason it takes the whole weekend is because you need Friday night to get ready, Saturday to participate and Sunday to recover.

- **Hiking Weekend.** Here's something that's within *any* family's reach, both in terms of finances and do-ability. Just pick a nearby scenic destination, put on good walking shoes (hiking boots if you'll be covering any challenging terrain), pack a picnic and plenty of water, and you're off. We're fortunate to live just minutes from the Tonto National Forest, so we try to hike as often as we can on the weekends. Again, don't expect everything to go perfectly. The very first time we hiked in Tonto as a family, we hadn't been on the path three minutes when Leah was "attacked" by a jumping cholla cactus. (These plants *really do* jump at you if you get too close.) Donna stood terror struck, looking at Leah's thorn-covered hand, while Leah screamed in pain. Fortunately, Cameron was more level-headed. He carefully plucked out each thorn, then looked Leah in the eye and asked her if she had the courage to press on. She did! And we headed into the desert with a healthy respect for cacti. It's a lesson Leah will always remember . . . and so will her parents.

Even if your "hike" is just a three-hour stroll through a local park, we think you'll be surprised at how reinvigorated everyone will feel. You might also be surprised at how much your children (especially your teenagers) have to say. Away from the daily grind and without the usual electronic distractions, parent-child communication blossoms. The key, of course, is to leave the friends and Walkmans at home.

In the first chapter, we told you how Nikki, now thirteen, first came to live with us. In the beginning, she didn't talk very much, especially about her past. (If you ever need a description of a sulky teenager, we can give you a vivid portrayal. Yikes!) When Nikki *did* talk, it was only to criticize us. Yet she portrayed her own family life as Ozzie and Harriet revisited. We didn't know what it was going to take to get through the barriers she had built up over the years, and we were feeling very discouraged.

When life settled down a bit after the first few weeks, we began getting back into our daily routine of walking after dinner. We noticed almost immediately that when we went for our nightly walks, Nikki would begin talking more openly and honestly. Since then, we've discussed this phenomenon with other families, and they've experienced a similar openness with their children. If you hike for no other reason, hike to *listen to your kids*. One word of warning: don't overdo it. Don't undertake a ten-mile nature walk with a two-year-old. A four-year-old should be able to survive a mile round-trip; a six-year-old about a mile and a half; and an eight-year-old, two miles. Of course, if you build up over time, you can increase these distances. Our six-year-old can easily walk two miles, provided the pace is reasonable. On a recent trip to Canada, she walked six miles per day. We know many adults who can't do that!

- **Nature Trips.** In the previous chapter, we introduced the concept of Nature Study and how it could be incorporated into your daily life. It can also make for a weekend find— if you don't take the whole thing too seriously. Remember, the idea is to *play together* and have fun. Shortly after we began reading Charlotte Mason, we realized that Leah could benefit from a trip to the famed Desert Botanical Garden in Phoenix. Since we wanted to help her along the way in developing her observation skills, we decided to act as her guides. After all, we had not previously taken all this nature business seriously enough, and she might just be falling behind. We can't have that now, can we?

From the moment we entered the garden, we were testing her on the various types of botanicals and drilling her on the varieties of cacti surrounding us. "This is a saguaro," we would say, trying to sound casual. "A saguaro looks like a man holding his hands in the air. Now, Leah, can you say saguaro? Good, show us another saguaro. Now this is an ocotillo. . . ." and so it went. It wasn't long before we realized that Leah (whom we nicknamed Nature Girl) absolutely HATED the illustrious Botanical Garden and, to tell you the truth, so did we. That didn't stop us though. We continued the cacti lecture for another miserable forty minutes, then finally surrendered. Defeated, we decided it was time to go home. A funny thing happened when we shut up. Leah discovered . . . the Botanical Garden.

On the side of the path was a hands-on exhibit, where children could pretend to be Native American squaws grinding mesquite beans into flour. We sat quietly while Leah ground pod after pod. If we would have let her, she would have stayed for hours. Near the exit to the garden, she found a small swamp teeming with frogs and tadpoles. She sat for nearly an hour, completely captivated. Several days later, we went to the library and picked out some books on frogs and tadpoles. That was more than a year ago, and she still fondly recalls her first encounter with tadpoles.

We had gone to the botanical garden to teach her how to identify cacti. When we let go of our agenda, stepped back, and let her interact directly with God's creation, magic happened. We promise it will be the same with your young children.

- **Fall Fun.** If there's one thing we really miss about the East Coast, it's the wonderful fall traditions. Oh, how we loved raking leaf piles to jump into! We think the invention of leaf blowers is downright sad. Raking is such great exercise and great "therapy," too. If you live in an area with four seasons, don't let the joy of fall pass you by. Get your whole family outdoors, roll up your sleeves, and have some family fun. Another great tradition we enjoyed was going on a hayride in a pumpkin patch, to pick out that special pumpkin or two (or three . . .). Now we pick our pumpkins at the grocery store. Ho hum. It just goes to show, "You don't know what you've got till it's gone." So, on behalf of the Partows, please make the most of the fall season's traditions. Last year we searched far and wide, but couldn't find a single hayride-and-pumpkin-pickin' spot in the entire Phoenix area. If you know of one, give us a call!

  When Donna was growing up, she lived near apple and peach orchards. She and her brothers and sisters would pick baskets filled with the fresh fruits, and Mom would make them into the most incredible homemade pies. You can easily adapt the tradition by visiting one of the "pick your own" farms that have sprouted up around the country. Here in Arizona, there are plenty of "pick your own" orchards . . . but does anyone know a good recipe for grapefruit pie? (By the way, if you substitute fructose for sugar when baking, you'll be committing a lesser dietary offense. Besides, the calories burned picking your own fruit will help offset the calories gained eating the fruit pie!)

  What about those of us who aren't lucky enough to be visited by fall's beauty? Here's an idea we're planning for this year. (We read about it in *Family Fun Magazine*. If you don't have a subscription, by all means, get one immediately. Each issue is jam-packed with fun and active ideas and the cost is only about $1.00 an issue. It's more than worth it. To order, call 800-289-4849.) Back to the great idea: No matter where you live, even on a tropical island, you can create that special fall atmosphere. Just convert your garage (or other suitable spot) into a barn for the weekend. Fill it with straw bales, pumpkins, and cornstalks. Add lanterns, an old saddle or two, and some down-home fiddlin' music. *Voila!* Instant festivity. Brew some piping hot cider, pop some corn, and you've got a harvest festival. Invite some neighbors and friends, and throw an old-fashioned barn dance. (By the way, there's a wonderful book for children, *Barn Dance* by Bill Martin, that you might enjoy reading aloud for inspiration.)

Getting Started

To get you started on the path to enjoying more active weekends, pick one of the ideas described above. In addition, the following list features fifty-two weekends worth of active ideas your family can try. Again, you might want to photocopy or re-create the list, cut out the items that appeal to your family and place them in a decorated can marked "Weekend Fun." When you run out of active ideas, pick one and run with it.

Fifty-Two Weekends of Active Fun

Plant a flower or vegetable garden
Weed a garden
Go camping
Take a hike
Visit a farmers' market
Visit a planetarium
Go on a nature walk, carefully observing, taking notes and
    sketching what you see
Have a picnic at a nearby park
Spend the day beachcombing

Build a tree fort
Redesign your backyard
Remodel your backyard
Visit the zoo
Go sledding
Hot air balloon ride
Ladies host an outdoor tea party
Backyard camp-out
Sleep under the stars (no tents)
Bonfire and sing-along on the beach (or lake, etc.)
Walk-a-thon
Bike-a-thon
Fun run
Scavenger hunt
Yard sale shopping for used sports equipment and other
    "active family" gear
Take a walking tour of historic sites
Take a walking tour of your city's cultural district
Canoeing
Kayaking
Cycling
White-water rafting
Camping
Climb a mountain (start with a small one!)
Backpacking
Family reunion
Neighborhood fitness festival
Attend a health fair
Set up/build an obstacle course
Have a car-free weekend: walk or ride bikes *everywhere*
Have an all-outdoor weekend
Research an old-fashioned weekend
Have an old-fashioned weekend
Square dancing
Barn dance
Birdwatching expedition

Horseback riding
Hayride
Fishing
Family marathon (activity of your choice)
Bowl-a-thon
Working weekend at a farm or ranch
Cross-country or downhill skiing
Attend an outdoor concert

The spirit is willing, but the body is weak.
—Matthew 26:41

Discussion Questions

1. Discuss each of the activities and highlight those that you would consider doing as a family.

2. Add additional ideas to the list.

Suggested Family Activities

1. Plan a mini-vacation for the near future. It doesn't have to be elaborate or expensive. How about a picnic, a hike, or a long bike ride? Note your plans below:

2. Reprint the ideas you like on slips of paper or cut them out of the book. Put them in a container labeled "Weekend Fun."

3. Draw a slip of paper and do what it says this coming weekend.

4. Plan to choose a slip of paper every Monday night at dinner, to determine what you will do each week.

Active Family Journal

It's not just the years in your life, but the life in your years that counts.

Describe your active weekend.

_____

_____

_____

_____

_____

_____

_____

_____

_____

_____

_____

_____

_____

_____

_____

_____

_____

_____

_____

_____

_____

_____

_____

_____

_____

_____

Chapter 4

CAMPING: THE "ORIGINAL" ACTIVE VACATION

Great things happen
when men and mountains meet;
Such things never happen
In the jostlings of the street.

—William Blake

Getting active outdoors is a great way to get in touch with God's creation. It's the kind of genuine recreation that enables the body, mind, and soul to experience a type of *re-creation* that many Americans have forgotten exists. Time spent outdoors has a close to miraculous way of putting the madness of everyday life into perspective, while calming the heart. As we gaze upon and contemplate the incredible majesty brought about by the hand of God, we will have renewed confidence to face life's challenges, knowing the same hands are those that hold us.

My first camping experiences were during elementary school. For two summers in a row, I attended a church-run youth camp, where we lived in cabins for a week, went hiking on well-worn trails through the nearby mountains, learned to canoe, swam in the not-so-crystal-clear lake, fought off bird-sized mosquitoes . . . and grew closer to God. And, well, I absolutely loved it. There was something genuinely awe-inspiring about being in the midst of God's creation (okay, so it wasn't exactly pristine, but it wasn't suburban Philadelphia and that's what mattered to me).

During the summer after I graduated from high school, I attended another church camp and again found myself drawn near to the God I had ignored since the summer camp days of my early youth. My high school years had been a blur of wild and crazy toga parties, drinking, doing drugs, and generally acting like a teenage lunatic. But in the mountains, away from my peer group and the other pressures of life, I was able to make a firm commitment to Christ, which I have followed to this day.

Later that same summer, a family at the church invited me to join them in the Adirondack Mountains for two weeks of tent camping. This time there were no formal programs—no chapel service, no small group Bible studies—just the unspoiled beauty of nature. And do you know . . . those two weeks were absolutely *life transforming*. No matter how cliché it may sound, there *is* something powerful and, yes, *spiritual* about the great outdoors.

We realize that not all families can handle the rigors of camping, but those who *can* seem to love it. Elissa, Werner, and Kelsey Wolf are a "camping family" here in our neighborhood, so we asked them to share their experiences:

> We both grew up in camping families, so it was a natural thing to start doing it together. We had gathered tents, stoves, camp boxes, and all the gear we needed over the years. When our daughter, Kelsey, came along, we didn't want her sleeping on the ground, so we decided to invest in a pop-up tent. We weren't sure we'd like camping in a trailer, because it's quite different, so we bought a cheap, ugly, smelly thing for $400 from a guy Werner worked with. It blew fuses in our truck every time we tried to hook it up. It was a true testimony of the fact that you get what you pay for. But it was enough to sell us on the concept of camping in a camper. Being a tent couple is one thing; a tent *family* is another ball of wax.

During the hot Phoenix summers, we try to get away as often as we possibly can. Camping makes for a good, inexpensive weekend getaway. There's so much to see in the mountains: different birds, different squirrels. Kelsey had never even seen a squirrel until we went camping! There's no telephone, no TV. We occasionally take a radio, but not usually. It's the only uninterrupted time we get together. If we stay home, Werner will cut the grass or change the oil. I'll paint or sew. You always find something you have to do when you're home. Camping forces us to spend time focusing on each other, which I think is really important.

We appreciate the peace and quiet. The only thing we hear are bees or birds flying by or the sound of the wind through the trees, otherwise it is completely silent. You can't help relaxing, and everybody needs that. It's a time to think about why you're doing what you're doing; a time for uninterrupted thought.

When you're camping, your family is your only priority. Once you get set up, you don't have to do anything except gather firewood and cook. Life is so simple. There's no reason to say [to Kelsey], "Not now, Mommy's busy." It forces me to spend quality time with her. I'm not looking at my house saying, "This place is a disaster." I'm not distracted. I just sit and spend time with her.

We decided we wanted to upgrade our camper, so we started watching the newspaper ads. We did a lot of research. We made a list of what features were necessary and which would be nice. One thing we needed was a bigger bed.

We eventually found a trailer through a classified paper for employees at Werner's job. One of his co-workers sold us a Coleman Rio Grande, with a queen-size bed, full-size bed for Kelsey, a table that turns into a bed, a sink, and a stove. It's still a pop-up, but it's a luxury pop-up. We paid around $4,000, which was below book value.

We know camping is not for everyone. One of our neighbors tried it, but when a tarantula crawled across her leg, that was the end of it! There's dirt everywhere, and you just get filthy and smoky. When you get back home, you've got tons of laundry and cleaning to do. We have a port-a-potty, which is fine for us, but some people would rather die than use one.

We find our own spots to camp rather than going to campgrounds. We don't like them because they are too crowded and noisy. We prefer a primitive environment. People at campgrounds usually try to recreate suburbia. If we're going to have people right next door, we can stay home.

We do have more fun when we camp with just one other family, though. We go with someone who has a child to play with Kelsey. It even helps if you forget something or don't have all the gear you'd like. It's nice to have friends to sit around the campfire with. They will have skills you lack—one can light the perfect fire, another can identify birds and animal species. Someone knows first-aid, someone else knows how to cook awesome camping food.

Camping Options

If the benefits of camping sound great, but you've never tried it before, resist the temptation to rush out and buy a bunch of equipment. Rent or borrow what you need for the first few outings before investing in stuff you'll end up selling at next year's yard sale. We bought our tent for $20 at just such a yard sale.

We also warn you against making your first camping expedition solo. Instead, team up with an experienced camping family and let them show you the ropes . . . and the stakes, poles, ground cloths, air mattresses, propane tanks, etc.

Another great option to consider is camping at national or state parks. We use the term "camping" broadly, because options range from campsites, teepees and rustic cabins, to historic lodges and luxurious hotels. Other alternatives to traditional camping include renting a cottage on a lake, a cabin in the mountains, or even a condo on the ocean—the key is getting close to nature and leading a simpler life, if only for a week or a weekend.

Organized Camping

If roughing it on your own sounds too challenging, you might consider a professionally-run family camp. You can enjoy the "camping" lifestyle without the headaches. The camp operators will organize and supervise activities, provide lessons in outdoor survival and, best of all, they'll even prepare all the food. Of course, it'll cost you a bit more: between $300 to $600 per person (everything included), but it's still cheaper than many other vacation options.

According to *U.S. News and World Report,* "Family camps are a genuine trend. In 1982, the American Camping Association's annual guide listed only 48 camps run either as family camps or as kids' camps open sporadically to families."* According to Bob Schultz, Director of Public Relations, the 1996 edition listed about 250 family-oriented camps and the number continues to grow annually. Call 800-428-2267 to order the guide ($16.95). The guide is also available on IBM-compatible diskette ($19.95) and can be accessed on the Internet at http://www.ata-camps.org.

Many churches and denominations sponsor an annual Family Camp, where they provide opportunities for spiritual growth, in addition to the joy of getting back to nature and taking a break from the daily routine. We know many families who consider church family camp the annual highlight of their summer.

Recreational Vehicle

When we decided to visit the Grand Canyon, we had lots of options about where to stay. There's a luxury hotel, a lodge, rustic cabins, campgrounds, you name it. We chose to travel by recreational vehicle (RV). It is definitely the way to go if you want to enjoy God's creatures without sacrificing your creature comforts. Our neighbor, Vince Meo, who owns Rainbow RV in Mesa, Arizona, graciously loaned us a 27-foot vehicle. This plushly carpeted RV included a bathroom (with shower), an eat-in kitchen (oven, stove, microwave, refrigerator, freezer, etc.), and enough sleeping room for six people.

---

*"Summer Camp Is for Parents, Too," (May 6, 1991), p. 68.

Buying an RV is a huge investment, with prices for a new vehicle ranging from $30,000 to $500,000, according to Vince. However, you can purchase a secondhand RV for significantly less. If you look at it as a life-time vacation investment, it begins to make more financial sense. Especially when you compare the alternative of investing in a vacation home. "The great thing about buying an RV is that you are getting a vacation-home-to-go," explains Vince. "You have all the advantages of a vacation home: the convenience and comfort of familiar surroundings. Plus you get the adventure of constantly exploring new locations. It's really the best of everything."

Another option is to rent an RV for a week (or more) from companies like CruiseAmerica, which has 100 locations around the United States and Canada. (Call 800-327-7799 for more information.) The cost ranges from $700 to $1,300, depending upon the time of year and the size (21 feet to 30 feet) of the vehicle. Although that's obviously much more than you'd spend on conventional camping, it's much less than you'd spend on the typical American vacation, complete with airline tickets, car rental, hotel bills, dining out, etc. When you compare options, it's actually quite affordable.

As Gwen Ellis notes in her book, *Finding Dollars for Family Fun*, recreational vehicles "give children a sense of stability while traveling. They sleep in the same bed every night, hang their clothes on the same hooks every day, and eat their meals at the same table, even though the vehicle may be parked in a different spot every day. This kind of routine avoids a lot of upset and confusion in their lives." Can you put a price tag on that?

One of the safest and most affordable places to get started with a camping adventure is at a state or national park. There are literally thousands of them around the country and they are filled with fun, affordable, active opportunities for your whole family. That's why we've compiled a state-by-state resource listing to help you discover these American treasures (see chapter 18). Happy camping!

God saw all that he had made, and it was very good.
—Genesis 1:31

Discussion Questions

1. Discuss the concept of camping.

2. Recount camping experiences you've had as a family or that Mom and Dad had growing up.

Suggested Family Activity

Plan a camping trip.

Active Family Journal

My father didn't tell me how to live; he lived, and let me watch him do it.

—Clarence Budinton Kelland

Record your response to your camping experience.

_____

_____

_____

_____

_____

_____

_____

_____

_____

_____

_____

_____

_____

_____

_____

_____

_____

_____

_____

_____

_____

_____

_____

_____

Chapter 5

ACTIVE VACATION FUN IN THE UNITED STATES

*There is one thing that remains constant through time:
the human need for the quiet solitude and beauty of
the wilds. Wilderness is not merely a nicety, it's a
necessity. Aside from the obvious relationship to clean
air, fresh water, and biological diversity, the
backcountry offers a spiritual cleansing essential to our
health and well-being. When you emerge from the
woods your thoughts are back in order, you are
refreshed, renewed, and invigorated.*

—Dave Wiggins, *American Wilderness Experience*

Over the past few years, "active travel" has become a booming business around the country (indeed, around the world) with some 10,000 travel companies in the U.S. alone. Active travel is a more moderate form of adventure travel, designed to include people of all ages, shapes, and physical conditions—not just the rugged, outdoor types.

You may be thinking: why should I bother with adventure or active travel? Can't we just go to an amusement park? Sure you can.

But we've noticed that "magic" happens when family members encounter and overcome nature's challenges together. It forms a very special bond. Imagine: you and your kids out for a day of rafting excitement along the Colorado River. You're meandering along the lazy old river, when boom! The rapids are upon you—white water as far as the eye can see. Suddenly, everyone in that raft knows: it's us against the elements. *Us.* What a wonderful word. If it's a word you don't hear much around your house, then maybe an active family vacation is just the ticket. Besides, we think all people need a little adventure in their life, especially people who don't understand why anyone would want adventure. Helen Keller said, "Life is either a daring adventure or nothing at all." And to be sure, any family with teenagers needs adventure. That's what teenagers are seeking, and they will find it one way or another. Why not give them positive adventure so they won't feel a need for destructive adventure?

This morning, our teenager, Nikki, left for a week at Summit Adventure, a Christian camp in California offering wilderness experiences with a view to changing lives. (This is her second year in their teen program; they also have programs for entire families, for fathers-and-sons, mothers-and-daughters, etc.) Dave Kelly, the camp director, explains their philosophy: "Through wilderness challenges, people tap into reservoirs of strength, insight, and confidence they can bring back home and apply to their day-to-day experiences. Our family programs are specifically designed to strengthen and build relationships centered on God, within the family unit."

Kelly says adventure camps offer people "a rare opportunity to leave their comfort zone behind and experience change in a way that helps them clearly define their identity, source of security, purpose, and direction in life. By combining radical acceptance of each individual with unprecedented challenge, we try to provide an environment where God can move people beyond their self-perceived limitations—whether spiritual, physical, mental, or emotional.

"I think kids of all ages need large doses of adventure in order to change, discover, and grow. If they aren't sufficiently challenged by positive, real-life adventures, they will seek out and find other fictitious adventures of significantly less value."

Those who provide active travel opportunities are called "outfitters" and they vary from flakes to fabulous. So be careful. The last thing you want is to find your family stranded in the middle of the Alaskan wilderness with a guide who has no idea where he's going, or with an outfitter who is trying to save money by providing inferior equipment or skimping on meals. The whole *point* of spending the extra money for a guided tour (rather than striking out on your own) is to minimize both the risks and the inevitable hassles.

If you want to truly enjoy your adventure, you have to trust your outfitter completely: to guide you, teach you, and handle all the logistics. And if they know exactly where the resident bald eagles have built their nests or the ideal time to spot elk grazing, so much the better. However, if you are second-guessing them every step of the way, your family *and* your outfitter will have a miserable time.

When you gear up for an active family vacation, one thing you absolutely *must* pack is a teachable spirit. If you take any of the vacations we suggest in this chapter, you'll have a lot to learn when you get there. Believe us, we know! From how to steer a canoe, to mounting a horse properly; from rappelling techniques, to how to lace your hiking boots to minimize blisters—everything is new. That's what makes it exciting! But it's also what makes active vacations potentially hazardous. So, travel with someone you trust to teach you along the way—and listen to his/her advice.

On most trips, in addition to "soft adventure" (as opposed to high-risk adventure), you will enjoy basic creature comforts, such as bathroom facilities (of one kind or another), and possibly showers (of one kind or another)! As a bonus, many outfitters offer exceptionally good food. Although many trips feature tent-sleeping only, it's also possible to find an active vacation featuring cabins, lodges, and country inns.

A good outfitter will pace the trip with a reasonable number of daily miles. They will understand that this is a vacation, not a marathon. If you are on the move, traveling from campsite to campsite (or cabin to cabin, etc.), they'll handle all the logistics. They'll figure out exactly how to move everything and everyone from Point A to Point B, without loading you down with a 90-pound backpack. Some people actually like backpacking, but we'd rather die. When we take a hike, a stick is the heaviest thing we want to carry. Outfitters rely on everything from horses and mules to hired hands and llamas to lighten the load. Backroads, which is one of the world's leading outfitters, has a van that travels the route carrying all the gear—and anyone who "poops-out" along the path.

Most of all, you want an outfitter who understands families and hires staff who LOVE children. A family-friendly outfitter will plan frequent breaks and quick, energy-boosting snacks throughout the day. But they won't plan every second; they'll allow for free time— time for talking and napping and bonding. And when you get to your campsite at the end of a long day, they'll do all the hard work, such as pitching the tents and building a fire. It would take you *hours*; they'll have it done in minutes. By the way, if you don't have a tent, sleeping bag, or other "adventure gear," most outfitters will rent it to you at a very reasonable price. One thing you will need to buy is suitable clothing, which will vary depending upon the type of trip you take.

We can't emphasize enough the importance of thoroughly investigating the outfitter before you embark on an active family vacation. Find out how long they've been in business, and talk with travel agents about their reputation in the industry. Once you have done that, here are eleven questions you should ask about your specific trip:*

1. How many people will there be on this trip? (Do you want an intimate atmosphere or a party atmosphere?)

2. Can you tell me about the backgrounds of those who've booked this trip (ages, genders, couples/singles/families)?

---

*"Eleven Questions to Ask an Outfitter," *McCall's* (March 1995), p. 106.

3. Can you give me references of people who've done this exact trip?

4. Will you accommodate a special diet?

5. How do I bathe/shower, and how often is this possible? What are the bathroom facilities like?

6. How much privacy or time alone will I have?

7. What's included in the total cost; what is not covered?

8. What kind of weather conditions can I expect?

9. What physical shape do I need to be in?

10. How are medical emergencies handled?

11. Is the outfitter bonded?

Listed below are some active vacation ideas, along with the names of reliable outfitters. Remember, there are literally thousands out there; we've only included those who have proven themselves over many years.

Biking/In-Line Skating

When we arrived at San Diego's fabulous Hotel del Coronado, our plan was to enjoy the bach life and take a nice, relaxing bike tour of historic Coronado Island. Well, we somehow managed to miss the leisurely bike tour's departure time, so our teenager persuaded us to go for the whirlwind in-line skaing tour instead. "Didn't you guys used to roller skate? It's the same thing. I'm sure you'll remember," she assured us.

Word to the wise: never trust a teenager. We knew we were in trouble when they made us sign medical release forms in quadruplicate. Then they brought out the gear. First the in-line skates—if you haven't tried them on, it's hard to imagine how *stiff* they are. The first thought that drifted through my mind was, "So this is what those knights in shining splendor felt like." My below-the-knee mobility factor was at sub-zero. But there was more, much more, to the suit of armor! Next came the knee pads. (Why do they call them "pads" as if we're dealing with soft cushy foam? They oughta be honest and call them shields.) Next came the elbow pads, then the wrist pads with the steel-reinforced hand guards. Last but not least, the helmet.

As I donned the gear, it occurred to me tht each piece had been developed *in direct response* to regulatory demand (or some similarly ominous reason). Bottom line: enough people had hazardous experiences in-line skating for an entire industry to spring up. This was not a comforting thought. I clung to the notion that "when it's your time to go, it's time to go anyway. May as well check out doing something glamorous."

Actually, there was nothing glamorous about my in-line skating style, but I trusted my family to embellish the tale if needed. My first mistake was agreeing to follow wherever our teenager chose to lead. She picked the route nicknamed "death by rollercoaster." I threw myself on the mercy of the grass and praised God for small hills. The only way poor Cameron could stay vertical was by clinging to Nikki. Whenever someone passed by, he'd pretend he was just giving her a pat on the back. We seriously doubt anyone was fooled. But, believe it or not, we decided to make it an "in-line skating vacation" and we actually DID get a little better at it.

"So this is . . . fun??" I asked Nikki. "I love it," she squealed. "When we get back, we should buy in-line skates. We can go all around the neighborhood. It's great exercise." Did you hear that, Moms and Dads? She said "we." That's the word you want to listen for; and that's the word you'll hear when you step out of your comfort zone. It's the *whole reason* we decided to become an active family.

When we weren't in-line skating, we were walking the beach, leaping over waves or—gulp—kayaking (more on that in a minute). We can't think of a more refreshing, beautiful place to try out the active family lifestyle than the Hotel del Coronado. (We can think of a lot of *cheaper* places . . . but if you want the vacation of a lifetime, this is the spot.

Hotel del Coronado
1500 Orange Avenue
Coronado, CA 92118

800-HOTEL DEL

If in-line skating sounds a bit ambitious and you'd like to try a less harrowing vacation on wheels, stick with bicycling. And if you really want to enjoy yourself, stick with one of the tried and true bike-trip outfitters listed below.

Backroads Bicycle Touring, Inc.
800-462-2848

Backroads has been offering biking tours around the country and around the world for decades. Their reputation in the industry is unparalleled. They offer weekend, week-long, and longer trips, many of them specifically for families.

Roads Less Traveled
P.O. Box 8187
Longmont, CO 80501
303-678-8750
800-488-8483

This outfitter specializes in low-pressure, family-friendly trips in the West. They offer inns, cabins, and camping, depending upon the trip you choose.

Dude Ranch

Our love affair with dude ranches started when our homeschool co-op did a study on horses. Inspired by all we were learning, we decided to take a trip to the famed Tanque Verde Ranch (800-234-DUDE) outside of Tucson. It's a historic working ranch and a four-star resort, combining the adventurous lifestyle of the Old West with all the amenities of a world-class resort. In short, it was right up our alley.

The ranch sits on 640 desert acres in the foothills of the Rincon Mountains, bordered by Saguaro National Monument and the Coronado National Forest. Although the ranch dates back to 1868, the facilities are quite modern: tennis courts, indoor and outdoor swimming pools, and a complete health spa. The food is abundant: we especially appreciated the piles of fresh fruits and salads they served up at the breakfast and lunch buffets. (We behaved so well at those two meals, we felt at liberty to break all the dietary guidelines at dinner, with scrumptious carrot cake and milk for dessert.)

First thing each morning, we'd hit the trail on trusty mounts we soon came to know by name. We immediately discovered that Leah "was a natural on horseback" as one of the wranglers put it. So after riding the trail, when Mom and Dad ran to soak their aching muscles in the hot tub, Leah stayed on for the "little wranglers" program, where she learned to trot, stop, and even steer her Palomino, named Ditto, around a barrel.

This impressive display had the whole family in awe—and Leah riding high in more ways than one. On the last day at the ranch, Leah and Ditto were among the horse-and-rider teams out for a "chuck wagon breakfast" in the desert. Leah not only controlled her own horse beautifully, she called back instructions to Mom's horse when it started misbehaving!

Then we heard about The Wickenburg Inn (800-942-5362) and since it was about 190 degrees in Phoenix (only a *slight* exaggeration), we decided to head to the high country to cool off. In Arizona, 100 degrees—the temperature in Wickenburg during our visit—is considered cooling off. The first thing that hit us was the magnitude of the place. It sits in the midst of nearly 5,000 wilderness acres with 100 horses and 60 head of cattle. From our casita on top of a hill, we could literally see for miles.

We looked at each other and said, "Now this is *City Slickers* come-to-life." We soon found out the resemblance to the movie was no accident. Apparently Hollywood's own Merv Griffin bought the place nearly a year ago and has poured a million dollars into upgrading it and making it, well, just like *City Slickers*. We didn't see any talk-show hosts or celebrities of any kind on our visit, which was probably for the best. I looked a mess. On the other hand, we *did* meet families from Austria, Switzerland, France, and Germany.

The Inn had such a contagious spirit of friendliness, we couldn't help becoming fast friends with both staff and visitors alike. What an exciting moment when we sat in the cozy lodge, watching the opening ceremonies of the 1996 Summer Olympics with people from around the world.

Another exciting moment was when Leah and I hit the trail on horseback and within minutes encentered a rattlesanke. The leathery old cowboy leading the charge said, "Turn those horses around." Being the cooperative type (not to mention the terrified-of-snakes type), I was quick to oblige. I turned that horse around, gave it a swift kick, and a half ton went a runnin' in the opposite direction. I soon regained my composure. What I *couldn't* regain was control of that horse. Mr. Cowboy was not at all pleased with this display and began yelling, "Lady, stop that horse" in a tone that let me know he had little patience for horsin' around. "I'm tr-r-r-r-r-y-i-n-g" came my earnest reply. I won't disclose all the embarrassing details. Let's just say if he hadn't come after me, I'd still be riding due north.

Leah later told me, "You shouldn't have been afraid, Mom. He was a friendly rattlesnake. He just wanted to come out of his hole to say hi. He even smiled at me." Frankly, I never want to get close enough to a rattler to determine whether he's smiling or frowning. That's not to say we let a little thing like near catastrophe spoil our adventure. Later that day, we were back out on the trail for the sunset ride. It was absolutely spectacular. Breathtaking. Just as we were returning to the ranch, the sun slipped behind the mountains and the sky turned radiant with color. As if they'd heard an alarm clock, the howls of a dozen coyotes went up throughout the desert. "Did you hear that?" "Did you hear that?" we asked each other, knowing full well it was impossible not to hear it. But some moments are so incredible, you just need to make sure you're not dreaming.

When we weren't horsin' around, we devoted ourselves to swimming, eating, talking, dreaming, and stargazing. As one Austrian girl remarked, "I have never seen the Milky *Path* so clear." (We'll be having fun with that Milky Path line for years!) She was right, though. Whoever said there's nothing like a Montana sky ain't been to Wickenburg, Arizona lately. We laid on the roof of our casita for hours at night, staring in awe at the magnitude and wonder of God's creation.

Another highlight was meeting Fred, the roadrunner, and dozens of skittish quail (you can't help wondering where they're hurrying off to all the time). And Leah had a blast chasing the giant jackrabbits, which looked more like miniature kangaroos than any cottontail we've ever seen. We even heard from a reliable source that "if only we'd been there a day earlier" we could've seen a mountain lion and her cub who stopped by for a visit. We weren't sure whether to be disappointed or relieved. But then, hey, it's all part of the Dude Ranch lifestyle. Try it. We think you'll like it, partner!

Tanque Verde Ranch
14301 East Speedway
Tucson, AZ 85748
800-234-DUDE

The Wickenburg Inn
P.O. Box P
Wickenburg, AZ 85358
800-942-5362

Colorado Dude & Guest Ranch Association
P.O. Box 300
Tabernash, CO 80478
303-724-3653
Offers a free directory of ranches who meet the quality/service standards of the association. It includes photos, maps, and information on the facilities activities offered at each ranch.

Old West Dude Ranch Vacations
(American Wilderness Experience)
P.O. Box 1486
Boulder, CO 80306

303-444-2622
800-444-0099

Every year, AWE publishes an up-to-date, state-by-state guide to dude ranches with complete descriptions, including photographs, maps, facilities, riding programs offered, and price information. See more information below under "rafting."

Hiking/Walking

Every year, I lose ten pounds during my week-long "walking vacation" in Vancouver, British Columbia. Unfortunately, it's always the *same* ten pounds. Nevertheless, I consider this yearly tradition an important part of my overall fitness regime. And it sure beats a "tradition" of eating hot dogs and soda at an amusement park! Even though it's not a formal "walking tour" such as those described below, we approach it with just as much enthusiasm and determination.

We stay at Cameron's parents' condominium just three blocks from the beach, but rather than lounging around on beach towels, we walk. And walk and walk—an average of ten miles per day. (In case you're wondering why we're not swimming, the ocean is always freezing, even in July. The Canadians don't seem to mind; but then again, just because polar bears swim in ice doesn't mean we're gonna try it!

We not only value this as a time to get our bodies into excellent condition, we use the time to talk and plan and dream. Most of our important life decisions have been made walking along the beaches and parks of Canada.

We hope you go walking or hiking every chance you get—right in your own neighborhood, or at nearby parks. If you fall in love with it, as we have, perhaps you'd like to make a vacation out of it. If that sounds like a boring vacation, then you haven't done your homework yet. There are a myriad of outfitters who offer wonderful hiking holidays all over the country and around the world. If your family has never attempted an active vacation before, this is the perfect way to start.

When you take a walking tour, you really get to know a region well—unlike when you drive by on a tour bus. Again, we would encourage you to request brochures from some of the outfitters listed below, to get a better picture (literally!) of what this type of active vacation is really all about. We think you'll be impressed.

Backroads Bicycle Touring, Inc.
800-462-2848
Don't let the name fool you; Backroads isn't just for biking. They have been offering hiking tours around the country and around the world for decades. Their reputation in the industry is unparalleled. They offer weekend, week-long, and longer trips, many of them specifically for families.

If you'd rather strike out on a walking vacation on your own, a great resource is the book *Walking*, by Ruth Rudner (Human Kinetics). It includes more than fifty pages of "The Best Places to Walk" in North America, Australia, and New Zealand, including full-color photos, maps, and where to go for further information. The book also offers tips on how to enjoy the walking experience with proper preparation, gear, and technique.

Llama Trekking

An increasingly popular active vacation, "Llama trekking" allows families with children (as young as four, depending upon the outfitter) to explore high mountains while a llama carries the supplies and camping gear. Basically, you walk the trail with your "own" llama on a rope behind you. Although we haven't tried llama trekking, llamas are well-known for their gentle temperament and sure-footedness. Most llama treks range from three to five days and are geared toward "couch potato" families. That is to say, you cover only about six miles per day—with plenty of stops and snacks along the way. Nevertheless, if you plan to go llama trekking (or any other kind of trekking) you'd be well advised to get in shape ahead of time.

Unlike the other active vacation ideas covered in this chapter, we are not aware of any regional or national outfitters, but here are some local companies with solid reputations:

- Great Northern Llama Company, Montana, 406-755-9044.

- Hurricane Creek Llama Treks, Oregon, 800-528-9609.

- Shasta Llamas, California, 916-926-3959.

- Telemark Inn Llama Treks, New Hampshire, 207-836-2703.

Water Sports (Rafting/Kayaking/Canoeing)

"Who wants to be the first to get in?" the tour guide asked cheerfully. One look at the huge bay and the tiny boat assured me of one fact: It wasn't gonna be Mom. Fortunately, Leah voluntered and quickly lowered herself into the waiting kayak. The "kayak boss" (as we affectionately dubbed him) gave her a little push off the dock and she promptly panicked. Back on shore within seconds, it was decided she would ride tandem with the boss. Had I known how physically demanding the next hour and a half was going to be, I would have been even *more* jealous.

I figured I'd hold out as long as possible . . . and pretended to be too enthralled with the beauty of Hotel del Coronado (our host for the tour of San Diego Bay) to lower myself into a teeny-tiny little kayak. Eventually there was only one empty kayak and one person left on deck. I took the hint and got on board. We were off. Nikki took to it right away; she also took to deliberately bumping into my kayak just to terrify me. Then a woman twice my age started literally paddling circles around me, smiling the whole time. Meanwhile, Leah sat on her perch at the front of the lead kayak, regaling the "boss" with stories of her fishes and turtle and bunny.

Speaking of fish, the guide casually announced that the water we were kayaking through was filled with stingrays and sharks. "Sharks?" I inquired, trying to sound just as casual. He detected my panic: "Sand sharks. They're harmless. Even if you capsize, and not many people do, you'll be fine." I was thinking about how many "not many" equalled, when Nikki announced the sighting of a ray. Leah said she couldn't wait to see a shark. In short, we were having fun!

At 8:30 A.M., the shores of the Bay were hopping with activity: bird activity, that is. Our guide pointed out a large heron, three pelicans, and a dozen terns, diving for fish. We even spotted the "rare and illusive" sea gull. Mostly, though, we enjoyed the peace and solitude of the water. As the morning wore on, we grew more comfortable in our kayaks and more confident of or paddling technique. I discovered I could make it farther faster if I threw my whole body into the stroke. Since I was perpetually "bringing up the rear," I didn't concern myself with how silly I might look.

When I climbed out of the boat, I gave another performance. This time acting like I *wanted* to remain seated on the dock chatting with the kids. The truth? I couldn't get up! To this moment, I have no idea why my *knees* hurt. I mean, I was paddling with my arms not my legs. But did they ever hurt! Of course, I found out what *real pain* was the next morning. I'd been meaning to add an "upper body workout" to my routine. Well, kayaking gave me the upper body workout of a lifetime.

If you think you'd like to try a kayaking, rafting, or canoeing vacation, my advice is: first, work on strength conditioning. Second, go with an experienced outfitter, so you can concentrate on navigating your boat—rather than the logistics of the trip. If you'd like to take short trips interspersed with professional massages to ease your aching muscles, we highly recommend "the Del." (The address is on page 66.) The kayak tour was only $24 and we thoroughly enjoyed it.

For weekend or week-long water sport vacations, contact:

Kayak & Rafting Expeditions
800-824-3795

Dvorak's has been around for a quarter-century, so if you're looking for an outfitter to provide a safe yet exciting water sport experience in the Midwest, they're a great choice. Trips run anywhere from two to six days and are rated from child-safe to extremely demanding.

Outdoor Adventure River Specialists (OARS)
800-346-6277
　　If you want to get the family excited about a kayaking or rafting trip, call for the OARS brochure. Even the most sulky teenager will get inspired. OARS is another well-established outfitter, with twenty-five-plus years in the business. They offer a range of trips, from easy to challenging, in various Western states. Float trips for four years old and up; mild rapids for ages seven and older.

Any Active Vacation

American Wilderness Experience (AWE)
P.O. Box 1486
Boulder, CO 80306
303-444-2622
800-444-0099
　　AWE is a clearinghouse and central reservation office for dozens of adventure travel outfitters offering more than 100 options, such as hiking, biking, river rafting, canoeing, cross-country skiing, kayaking, and dude ranches. AWE's President, Dave Wiggins, says, "We like people to call and tell us what they're looking for, and then we can suggest the type of vacation that's just right for their needs. We're here to prescribe the ideal antidote for the stress and craziness of an over-civilized world!" They've been in the active travel business for twenty-five years, and they know which outfitters are reputable and which are not. We have used AWE to plan a dude ranch vacation, so we can personally vouch for their professionalism. Ask for their Catalog of Domestic and International Backcountry Travel or their Old West Dude Ranch Vacation Guide. When you call, be sure to tell Dave we sent you.

Getting Started

Okay, you and the kids are ready to head out for an excellent adventure. Where do you begin? Contact some of the outfitters listed in this chapter and ask for their brochures. Most of them have beautiful full-color materials that will have your family dreaming big dreams and bursting with enthusiasm for the ultimate trip. One of our top goals as a family is to travel the world, experiencing every *type* of travel imaginable. We want to do it all, from llama trekking to white water rafting and everything in between. Hey, that's our family identity now. "We're an active travel family."

Our teenager loves looking at the travel brochures, talking about all the places she's going to visit and the daring things she's going to do when she gets there. And how she can just imagine us making fools of ourselves at every turn. (You know, teenagers always think their parents look foolish, even when we think we're lookin' good!) Just last night, we let Leah look through old brochures (once you're on these mailing lists, you get tons of brochures) and told her to cut out pictures of all the destinations she wanted to visit. She cut out *every* picture. Mom and Dad cheered, "Amen."

If you suspect that those travel brochures may not exactly offer you an unbiased perspective, you're right. So do some additional homework. (Hey, it's *fun* homework. The kind of homework your kids will LOVE doing.) Two excellent resources we've uncovered are *Family Travel* by Evelyn Kaye (Blue Penguin Press, $19.95. Call 800-800-8147) and *Adventure Travel North America* by Pat Dickerman (Adventure Guides, $16.95. Call 800-252-7899).

Family Travel is a 200-page handbook listing hundreds of active vacation ideas for families of all ages. The book is divided into vacation categories, such as camping, rafting, hiking, biking, nature trips, farms, and dude ranches. Evelyn Kaye has done it all with her own family and her guidance is invaluable if you haven't yet experienced an adventure vacation but want to give it a try. Along with a basic overview of each type of adventure, Kaye lists specific outfitters whom she has investigated and who have established a record of successful family vacations around the world.

For each outfitter, she describes at what ages children are accepted and the best age to come; a detailed list of what's included in the price; the equipment you'll need to bring along; what the accommodations and meals will be; and generally, what you can expect the trip to be like. If you plan to become an "active travel family," this book should be your first investment.

Adventure Travel North America does not offer as much *advice*, but once you've decided on the type of trip that's right for your family, it offers a much more comprehensive listing (in fact, *thousands* of adventures. So this will be your *second* investment). Categories range from hiking, biking, kayaking, and skiing to cattle drives, covered wagons, and fly fishing expeditions. Many of the listings include full-color photographs. Best of all, each category provides a state-by-state listing of outfitters, making the handbook much easier to use.

Another great resource is the *Destinations America CD-ROM* from Parsons Software (800–223–6925). Whether you want to ski the Rockies, sun yourself in Hawaii, or explore history in New England, you can use this software program as your "multi-media travel encyclopedia." The program covers all fifty states, and you can search by region, state, attraction type. You can even search for family-friendly destinations. Includes thousands of attractions and activities. It not only features thousands of color photographs, it has more than 100 videos! This is a really valuable resource. And it only costs $19. Check it out!

> *But those who hope in the* LORD *will renew their strength.*
> *They will soar on wings like eagles; they will run and not*
> *grow weary, they will walk and not be faint.*
> —Isaiah 40:31

Discussion Questions

1. Discuss the concept of adventure or active travel.

2. Invite everyone to suggest something adventurous they would like to try.

Suggested Family Activity

Investigate a family adventure, starting with the resources listed in this chapter.

Active Family Journal

The traveler is active; he goes strenuously in search of people, of adventure, of experience. The tourist is passive; he expects interesting things to happen to him. He goes "sight-seeing."

—Daniel J. Boorstin

Record your reaction to the concept of taking an active family vacation.

Chapter 6

ACTIVE VACATIONS AROUND THE WORLD

The world is a book, and those who do not travel read only a page.

—St. Augustine

Paul and Diane Davison of Bethlehem, Pennsylvania, and their two children, Whitney, seventeen, and Lindsey, seven, traveled to Costa Rica for two weeks in June 1994. "We had heard a lot about Costa Rica and had a strong interest in the environment," says Diane. "We wanted to see the rain forest firsthand. Our tour group (Family Explorations) made it easy to include our children and to expose them to a really different culture. They took care of everything for us and supplied some respite in the form of a counselor to take care of the children.

"We had done the typical amusement park vacation. We wanted something different, and this was the most daring thing we'd ever done. One of the neat things was that we went to different areas of the country. Our guide pointed out the foliage in a way the kids could understand, but still made it interesting for us. We also saw the damp and green rain forest and the cloud forest, which was high in the mountains. We even got to see an active volcano crater."

Diane explains, "It wasn't too demanding for the kids, but we weren't sitting around either. We went horseback riding for two hours, and my six-year-old hung right in there with it. Sharing those really unusual experiences created a certain kind of bond. Our kids think it is so neat that we went someplace where none of their friends have ever gone. Their friends think we're really cool parents, and that makes our kids feel good."

Another advantage, according to Diane, "The kids are more aware of the world around them. They saw other people live differently than the way we do, so they appreciate what they have at home. That was especially true in Central America. Driving through the countryside, seeing how people lived, how little they have. I know my daughter is a different person than she would be if she'd never left the American shores.

"So many people don't travel with their children, because they think they won't remember it and therefore it's not worth anything—not worth spending any money on it. I know that even though they may not remember exactly what happened, or exactly what adults remember, these experiences absolutely affect them. And it is absolutely worthwhile. There's nothing better for a kid than to travel. The best money a parent can spend is to take their children places and let them have these experiences."

She does add a word of warning: "I'd never take a child anywhere there might be danger, violence, or disease, but most of the world is quite safe. It's important to go with a tour who knows what they are doing, especially in non-European countries."

We love looking through bright colorful brochures, dreaming of the international vacations we will someday take. If you are looking for inspiration, try some of our favorites: Natural Habitat Catalog of Worldwide Nature Vacations (800-543-8917); Overseas Adventure Travel (800-221-0814); Country Walkers (800-464-9255); and Backroads (800-GO-ACTIVE). The most important rules to keep in mind are: Choose companies that SPECIALIZE in family travel, and remember that your children should be at least eight years old, well-trained, and *very* obedient. An unruly child will be a danger to himself and others. Here are some other tips:

Tips for Adventure Travelers

1. **Understand what adventure travel really is.** Adventure travel is an active, unique exploration of an exotic or remote destination with a small group of like-minded people, guided by full-time professional leaders. The typical object of your exploration is a beautiful landscape, unusual wildlife, or an intriguing foreign culture—often all three. You'll probably travel by foot, safari jeep, or dugout canoe, and over rough roads or trails in all kinds of weather. Exceptional physical fitness usually isn't necessary; you can enjoy some adventure trips at a fitness level only a notch or two above that of a couch potato. But you'll almost certainly get sweaty, dusty, and tired at times, and you won't be eating much *boeuf bourguignon*.

2. **Don't panic at the idea of camping.** Accommodations on adventure trips range from two-person tents to small rustic inns, to luxurious lodges. (Some trips have all three.) If you've never slept outdoors before, or if your previous camping experience wasn't much fun, remember that adventure-travel camping is ordinarily much easier than the usual do-it-yourself, backpack-style camping. Tented safaris in Africa can be downright luxurious, with huge stand-up tents, real beds, and hot showers. Even on more rugged camping-style trips, porters or pack animals usually carry the camping gear, your tent is often set up for you, and the camp staff does all the cooking and cleanup. But if camping just isn't your cup of tea, there are plenty of trips that offer lodges, rustic inns, houseboats, or local homestays.

3. **First pick a destination.** The vast number of adventure trips to choose from can be a bit bewildering. To narrow down the choices to a manageable number, decide early what part of the world you want to visit. If you're new at adventure travel and not quite sure where you want to go, pick a trip that has a track record of broad appeal over the years. Instead of, say, hang gliding with cannibals in Irian Jaya, stick to the classics: a safari in East Africa, a trek in the Himalayas, or a visit to the Amazonian rain forest.

4. **Decide how much physical challenge you want.** There's an adventure trip for virtually every level of physical fitness. Companies usually rate their trips as easy, moderate, or demanding. Study the trip ratings carefully; different companies use different rating criteria, based on the level of physical activity, altitude, and terrain.

   "Easy" trips usually include African safaris and cultural/nature-oriented trips, where hikes are optional and the camping, if any, is in a luxurious style. Rougher overland trips with long driving days and more optional hiking might be rated "easy/moderate." A full-fledged "moderate" trip often entails at least four or five days of camping and four to six hours of hiking per day over not-too-difficult terrain at altitudes below 15,000 feet. A "demanding" trek typically involves longer days, steeper terrain, and altitudes up to 19,000 feet. To enjoy a demanding trip, you should have made exercise a regular part of your life. Even on a demanding trek, however, you usually won't be carrying anything more than a light daypack.

5. **Decide how much variety you want.** Some people prefer to stay in one area so they can get to know it intimately, while others like to sample a wide variety of places and activities.

6. **Decide on your price range.** At a minimum, you'll probably spend about $2,000 per person, including airfare, for a ten-day trip. Longer trips to destinations like Asia or Africa cost $3,000 to $6,000, including airfare.

7. **Shop around.** Call several adventure-travel companies and request detailed itineraries for trips that interest you. For similar trips by different companies, compare trip routing and accommodations. Be sure to ask about potential extra costs like internal airfares, national-park fees, or pre- and post-trip hotels and meals. Go to the library and search the magazine databases for articles on the various travel companies you are considering, to get an objective review of the strengths and weaknesses of the various providers.

8. **Check out the trip leader.** The most important single factor

on an adventure journey is the trip leader, who simultaneously fills the role of guide, interpreter, teacher, mother hen, drill sergeant, and group counselor. A great leader can be an American expatriate or a well-qualified local citizen, but he or she should be a year-round resident of the country/region you plan to visit, and speak both English and the local language(s) well.

9. **Get in shape.** Physical requirements vary greatly according to the trip, and you should follow the guidelines in the pre-trip information your travel company supplies. But at a minimum, you should exercise briskly for at least twenty minutes, three times a week, for two months before departure. Walking or jogging is ideal, but an exercise bicycle or treadmill is a reasonable alternative. For hiking or trekking trips, stretch your walks to a couple of hours and spend extra time walking up hills, or join a health club and use the stair machine. Wear your daypack and fill it with ten to fifteen pounds to simulate a typical load on the trail.

Another good exercise idea is the roll-up, or crunch, which strengthens the stomach muscles and thereby reduces the risk of back problems. Lie on your back, with feet flat on the floor and knees angled at 90 degrees. Then, with hands behind your head, raise your torso as far as you can.

10. **Thoroughly break in your hiking or walking shoes.** Many first-time adventure travelers buy new hiking boots for the trip. You must walk a minimum of twenty miles in them, up and down hills, before departure. This should be enough to get over the initial break-in blisters and to ensure that they fit properly. Wear your new boots or shoes during your get-in-shape hikes.*

One resource worth checking out is the *Ultimate Adventure Sourcebook*, compiled by the staff of the Adventurous Traveler Bookstore ($29.95. Call 800-282-3963). This full-color, 432-page book covers everything from African safaris to white water rafting.

---

*Adapted with permission from the booklet "101 Tips for Adventure Travelers," published by Overseas Adventure Travel (800-221-0814).

The book rates guide services for quality, and includes recommended itineraries and trip prices. Not just a reference manual, it features over 400 superb color photographs from the world's top photographers. Purchasers of the book also qualify for substantial discounts with many of the top guide services mentioned in its pages.

"But you don't understand. I have kids!" you cry. We recommend that you check out *Adventuring With Children*, by Nan Jeffrey, with Kevin Jeffrey (Foghorn Press). The Adventurous Traveler Bookstore (800-282-3963) calls it "the how-to manual every family needs to enjoy any vacation involving hiking, sailing, biking, and international travel. It features low-cost travel and offers lots of practical insight on safety, keeping kids happy, and making the most of a budget. Of all the books available on travel with children, this is by far the best."

If you think you are ready for an excellent *international* adventure, following is a brief listing of fun, active vacations around the world. We have only listed companies which have earned a well-established, solid reputation in the field of international adventure travel. It goes without saying that you should personally investigate any travel company before investing your money and *entrusting them with your family's lives*.

AFRICA

Family Explorations
800-WE-GO-TOO

Family-friendly nature and cultural tours of South Africa featuring complete children's programs. From $2,000 to $4,000, depending upon the package you choose.

GEO Expeditions
800-351-5041

GEO Expeditions has arranged safaris for over a decade. Countries include Botswana, Kenya, Namibia, Tanzania, and Zimbabwe.

Accommodations range from tents to luxurious resorts, depending on your budget and preference.

Natural Habitat
800-543-8917
"Biological Journeys" emphasizing wildlife viewing and environmental understanding/awareness. *Offers special trips geared to families.* Countries include Botswana, Kenya, Namibia, Tanzania, Uganda, and Zimbabwe. Prices in the $3,000 to $5,000 range.

ASIA AND THE PACIFIC

Backroads
800-GO-ACTIVE
This group offers biking, walking, and hiking tours. Countries toured include China, Bali, Thailand, New Zealand, Australia, and Indonesia. Known for their distinctive lodgings and superior food. Most trips are in the $2,000 range.

EUROPE

Backroads
800-GO-ACTIVE
Biking and walking tours of countries including England, France, Ireland, and Italy. Accommodations range from French chateaux and Italian villas, to Irish castles and English manors. Known for their distinctive lodgings and superior food. Most trips are in the $2,000 range.

Country Walkers
800-464-9255
Unlike the more "adventure" oriented tour companies, they specialize in walking tours geared to all levels of fitness. Countries include Austria, England, France, Greece, Ireland, Italy, Scotland, Spain, and Switzerland. Most trips are under $2,000.

Family Explorations
800-WE-GO-TOO

Family-friendly nature and cultural tours featuring complete children's programs in Ireland and Italy. This tour costs around $2,000.

SOUTH AND CENTRAL AMERICA

Backroads
800-GO-ACTIVE

Offers biking, walking, and hiking tours. Countries toured include Argentina, Belize, Chili, Costa Rica, and Mexico. Known for their distinctive lodgings and superior food, most trips are in the $1,000 to $2,000 range.

Country Walkers
800-464-9255

Unlike the more "adventure" oriented tour companies, they specialize in walking tours geared to all levels of fitness. Countries include Chile, Costa Rica, Mexico, and Peru. Most trips are under $2,000.

Family Explorations
800-WE-GO-TOO

These family-friendly nature and cultural tours feature complete children's programs. Countries include Belize, Costa Rica, and Ecuador. Prices are in the $1,000 to $2,000 range.

Natural Habitat
800-543-8917

"Biological Journeys" emphasizing wildlife viewing and environmental understanding/awareness. *Offers special trips geared to families.* Countries include the Bahamas (for dolphin and whale watching), Costa Rica, Ecuador (Galapagos Islands), and Mexico. Most trips run in the $2,000 to $3,000 range.

Overseas Adventure Travel
800-221-0814

Hiking and boating tours of countries including Bolivia, Brazil, Chile, and Costa Rica. Accommodations range from hotels and country inns to adobe homes and jungle lodges. Most trips last ten to fifteen days and cost between $2,000 and $3,000 per person.

POLAR REGIONS

Natural Habitat
800-543-8917

"Biological Journeys" emphasizing wildlife viewing and environmental understanding/awareness. *Offers special trips geared to families.* Explores both North and South Pole regions, with trips to Alaska, Northern Canada, Norway, and Antarctica. Prices are in the $2,000 to $4,000 range. Expedition Voyages to Antarctica cost from $7,000 to $11,000.

Discussion Questions

1. Would you consider going on an overseas adventure? What might be the pros and cons for you?

2. What country in the world would you most like to see? Why?

Suggested Family Activity

Begin dreaming about the country you might someday visit. Send for catalogs, cut out pictures, have fun!

Active Family Journal

Take only photographs
Leave only footprints.

—National Park Service motto

Record your dreams and goals for a future family adventure overseas.

Chapter 7

SURVIVING ON THE WAY TO YOUR ACTIVE DESTINATION

"Are we there yet?"

One reason people don't travel to active destinations is because they dread the road trip. That was our attitude. The truth is, what happens in the car says much about your family: who you really are and the true status of your interpersonal relationships. We recently read an article suggesting parents buy a Walkman for each family member before taking a road trip, so the children won't fight, communicate, or otherwise function as a family unit. We think they missed the point, don't you?

Yes, it can be frustrating, aggravating, and downright unbearable. But it is absolutely vital for you to find out what is really going on in your family, and there's nothing like hours alone together in a car to get at the truth. Don't drown out the truth, deal with it— even if it is painful. In fact, especially if it is painful. Perhaps you can take notes concerning what you discover about your family's relationships, attitudes, etc., as you travel to your active destinations. Mom and/or Dad might want to keep a daily journal, in which they record:

- What did I learn about my family today?

- How does each family member respond to boredom?

- How does each family member respond to unexpected changes?

- How do family members treat each other?

- Do we enjoy each other's company?

- What does each child know that I didn't think he or she knew?

- What doesn't he or she know that I thought he or she did?

- How well does our family function as a team?

Surely you can think of other questions to ponder, as well. When you get back from your trip, debrief with your spouse and then seek to deal with the core problems you uncovered. In short, a road trip provides a rare opportunity, so don't miss it, *prepare* for it. By the way, if you don't prepare, that says something important about your family as well. Think about it.

Of course, all of this isn't to say you should deliberately make your time on the road as miserable as possible to ascertain your family's true character. A wise parent will seize the chance to *play together*. Here are some tips for doing just that:

- Consider traveling at night. Depart after dinner and let the children sleep.

- OR hit the road very early (perhaps by 5 A.M.).

- Set realistic limits on how many hours per day you plan to drive (we think eight is enough).

- When planning, factor in additional time for detours, lousy roads, rainstorms, etc. Don't put your family in a situation where you have to "push" to make it to your destination.

- Consider going to *one place* and staying there. Rather than trying to see the entire California coastline in a week, get a campsite or cabin in Yosemite. In other words, remember that vacations are for *relaxing* not for *running your family ragged*.

In her book *Finding Dollars for Family Fun*, Gwen Ellis writes, "I recently read an article that talked about the difference in American and European vacations. Americans tend to keep on the move while vacationing. I remember seeing a funny cartoon where a family had stopped at Yellowstone Falls in Yellowstone Park. One person in the family was snapping a picture, and a child sitting in the car was asking, 'What is it?' The answer was, 'I don't know, but I've taken a picture. We'll look at it and figure it out when we get home.' That's too true to be funny. It's all too typical of American vacations. Run! Run! Run! On the other hand, Europeans tend to go to one location and stay there for three or four weeks." Take your cue from our more "civilized" brethren across the ocean. Slow down!

- STOP and smell the roses along the way. Stretch your legs, play Frisbee, have a picnic, check out the local scenery. Don't rush to get "there"; enjoy the journey.

- Stay at hotels with swimming facilities—nothing rejuvenates kids like water play and nothing provides a better night's sleep, either. (It goes without saying that you should make *advance* reservations. Nothing could be worse than driving past one "No vacancy" sign after another when the whole family is exhausted.)

- Let one parent sit in the back. This will reduce backseat bickering and give both parents a chance to get to know the children better.

- Plan car activities (see below). Don't assume your children can amuse themselves for eighteen hours—they can't. When our good friends the Staffords traveled from Phoenix to Ft. Lauderdale last year with their two preteens, they tackled the project of listening to the complete *Pilgrim's Progress* on tape. Debbie, the mom, prepared in advance by developing discussion questions for each chapter.

- Bypass the fast-food restaurants and look for local, family-oriented restaurants. You'll eat healthier, learn more about the local culture, and build memories in the process. And remember to pack a small ice chest with carrots, celery, fruit, etc. Perfect for munching in between stops.

Discussion Topics for the Road

Why not look at your car trip as an exciting opportunity to capitalize on your captive audience? Talk to your children and genuinely *listen* to them. Here are some topics to get you started:

- Recount a book you've read or a movie you've watched recently.
- Tell tall tales.
- Recall (or create) family legends.
- Play "It could be worse. . . ." When things go haywire, make up outlandish examples of how the situation could actually be worse. (Well, don't get morbid!)
- Take turns telling Bible stories from memory.
- Recite as many Bible verses as you can from memory.
- Memorize Scripture verses.
- Memorize poems.
- Recite poems.
- Have a spelling bee (pack a small dictionary).
- Start a story and keep it going, taking turns adding to it.
- Tell stories from your childhood.
- Memorize an entire chapter of the Bible.
- Listen to the Bible on tape.
- Listen to uplifting praise music.

Backseat Travel Tote

Buy a plastic shoe bag and fill it with safe, quiet games and toys your children can play with in the backseat, as well as a few items to keep things clean and neat. Hang it from the back of the front seat. Here are some ideas:

crayons
coloring books
kids' magazines
craft supplies
magnetic checkers
miniature board games (now widely available)
pipe cleaners (kids can twist them to create stick figure people, animals, flowers, etc.)
paper doll kit
deck of cards
Brain Quest cards (Workman Press) K through 7
cassette player with read-along story tapes
paper and pencil for tic-tac-toe and hangman
wet towelettes, tissues, and paper towels
small trash bags

Rest-Stop Survival

Frisbee
jump rope
ball
nature notebook
birdwatching journal
nutritious food-to-go

Let each child buy one postcard at every rest-stop. If weather permits, gather round the picnic table (or spread a blanket) and let each person write down the most memorable thing that has happened since the last rest-stop. When you get home, hole punch the upper left-hand corner of the cards, and tie a ribbon through them. Voila! You've got an instant vacation journal. If you have a video camera, you can create a video journal, interviewing each member along the way.

License Plates From Every State

This is a favorite of many families. Cut out or photocopy this chart to use as a checklist. When you see the state's license plate, check it off.

☐ Alabama		☐ Montana	
☐ Alaska		☐ Nebraska	
☐ Arizona		☐ Nevada	
☐ Arkansas		☐ New Hampshire	
☐ California		☐ New Jersey	
☐ Colorado		☐ New Mexico	
☐ Connecticut		☐ New York	
☐ Delaware		☐ North Carolina	
☐ Florida		☐ North Dakota	
☐ Georgia		☐ Ohio	
☐ Hawaii		☐ Oklahoma	
☐ Idaho		☐ Oregon	
☐ Illinois		☐ Pennsylvania	
☐ Indiana		☐ Rhode Island	
☐ Iowa		☐ South Carolina	
☐ Kansas		☐ South Dakota	
☐ Kentucky		☐ Tennessee	
☐ Louisiana		☐ Texas	
☐ Maine		☐ Utah	
☐ Maryland		☐ Vermont	
☐ Massachusetts		☐ Virginia	
☐ Michigan		☐ Washington	
☐ Minnesota		☐ West Virginia	
☐ Mississippi		☐ Wisconsin	
☐ Missouri		☐ Wyoming	

(Hint: My editor claims you can win this game by driving through the parking lot at a major city zoo. Give it a try! If that doesn't work, try restaurant parking lots in Arizona during the "snow-bird" season. That might do it!)

See It All

Prepare a list of things for your children to sight (customize it based on what you expect to see) and have them check off the items as they find them. Here are some ideas to get you started:

school bus
deer
rabbit
road sign (specific)
MPH signs
Volkswagen bug
cows
horses
license plates (particular one)
billboards
sports activities
bicyclists
gas station signs

Foods to Avoid (if you want to stay sane)

No matter how tempting it is to indulge your tastebuds, you can be certain your vacation will be more enjoyable for all if you absolutely, positively ban the following:

soda
candy
cookies
milk products
fatty or fried foods
other foods that may cause allergic reactions

In short: avoid fast food restaurants and convenience stores. Instead, look for farmers' markets and home-spun restaurants.

Add your pet peeves to the list and carry it with you. Post it on your visor or dashboard. Then make a rule: Anyone caught eating or begging for items on the above list will suffer specific consequences (think up some fun but tough ideas).

Kids' Stuff

Here are two excellent resources for surviving on the road:

Family Travel (Focus on the Family) 800-A-FAMILY.

This travel bag includes a coloring/activity book, a sing-along cassette tape, and a laminated travel Bingo game (before you can yell "Bingo," you have to spot things like a church, barn, train, factory, horse, motorcycle, etc.). We used the Family Travel bag on a recent trip to California, and the kids gave it a thumbs up.

Travel Games for the Family, by Marie Boatness (Canyon Creek Press) 602-585-3059. $6.95.

This fun book really is filled with "100 ways to entertain kids of all ages for hours" as the sub-title promises. It includes action games, guessing games, alphabet and word games, art, music, and sound games, plus detective contests and math-skill builders. Each listing indicates the number of players needed, suggested ages and supplies (most require only paper and pencil, or nothing at all).

Keep a Positive Attitude

Remember that the journey is just as important as the destination. Too often, we're obsessed with getting "there" as quickly as we can so the vacation can start. The truth is, the vacation starts the minute you hop in that car. I think Cameron drives too slow (anything under 70 mph is a crawl, in my book) and it makes me nuts. I, in turn, do everything within my power to make him nuts.

On a recent four-hour road trip with our eight-week old baby in tow, I was determined we were going to "make good time." So I bugged and pestered and pleaded with Cameron to get with the program and press the pedal to the metal. I gave him moment-by-moment updates on the changing speed limits and a blow-by-blow analysis of his driving skills (never anything *positive*, you can be sure). In short, I made a four-hour trip absolutely miserable—all so we could arrive a bit sooner. Does this make sense??

Take my advice and in this case—do as I say (well, do as I *write*), not as I did. Keep a positive attitude, and don't worry about arriving thirty minutes later than you possibly could have. Better a *pleasant* four-and-a-half-hour drive than a *miserable* four-hour drive. Reread this last paragraph before you set off on your next road trip. I have promised my family *I* will.

> *Fathers, do not exasperate your children.*
> —Ephesians 6:4

Discussion Questions

1. Discuss your previous experiences on-the-road. Think back and try to recall what you learned about your family through those trips.

2. Encourage the children to offer suggestions for making future road trips more enjoyable.

3. Develop a Travel Rules list that everyone will agree to abide by.

Suggested Family Activities

1. Take a road trip and use the suggested activities and guidelines.

2. Have both parents (and possibly even older children) maintain a travel journal. When you return, compare notes.

3. Call a family meeting to discuss your conclusions—what's good in your family and what needs work.

Active Family Journal

Afoot and lighthearted I take to the open road,
Healthy, free, the world before me,
The long brown path before me leading
wherever I choose.

—Walt Whitman

Record your reaction to the road trip experience.

Part II: Fitness

FAMILIES THAT PLAY TOGETHER GET FIT

Research on children and physical activity shows the crucial role that parents play. More active parents have more active preschoolers, more active preadolescents, and more active adolescents. Parents who want their children to be active should follow three cardinal rules: set a good example; play together whenever you can; encourage and support children's participation in all kinds of physical activities.

—Gordon W. Stewart, author of *Active Living*

Chapter 8

WHY FAMILIES THAT PLAY TOGETHER STAY FIT

*You don't have to suffer to feel good. You can make
exercise a "playout" instead of a workout.*

—Dr. Dean Ornish

Have you noticed that a lot of kids seem to be in very bad physical
shape? If so, it's not just your imagination. The President's Council
on Physical Fitness and Sports agrees with your observation and can
back it up with statistics. "When the Presidential Physical Fitness
Award was given in 1976, 15 percent of high school students qualified. In 1983, the same test was given to 84,000 students and less
than one percent of those tested qualified" (*Homemade Health*).
Only 42 percent of American kids can pass the same fitness tests
that 92 percent of Europeans kids can pass (*Staying Thin*).

If your kids are like most school-aged children, they have developed a whole array of unhealthy habits. They spend an average
of 26 hours in front of a TV and 25 to 30 hours sitting in a desk each
week (*Chatelaine*, October 1994). Now add in car time, bus time,
phone time, then factor in sleeping time, and your children probably spend at least 70 percent of their lives either sitting or lying
down. It's not a very fit picture.

Our daughter Leah has a good friend on the local swim team,

and she invited us to attend one of her swim meets. We were expecting to see dozens of healthy, fit kids. Instead, we were astonished by how many of the children on the team were flabby and overweight. Although we didn't tabulate the statistics, our overall sense was that more children were overweight than not. *And these were the kids on the swim team!*

A poll conducted for *Prevention Magazine* by Louis Harris found that kids today are more likely to be overweight than ever before:

- Thirty-four percent of all kids ages three to 17 were overweight.
- Boys are more likely to be overweight than girls; 39 percent of boys; 30 percent of girls.
- Older kids are chubbier than younger kids: 22 percent of kids 12 years and younger are overweight; 57 percent of kids 13–17.

Isn't that last statistic incredible? More than *half* of America's teenagers are overweight. Unfortunately, 80 percent of overweight children will become overweight adults* and overweight adults are at increased risk for virtually *all* the major health ailments plaguing our country. As Ann Landers once wrote, "People spend the first half of their life learning habits that shorten the other half." It doesn't have to be that way for your children.

Having read the first part of *Families That Play Together Stay Together*, we hope you're inspired by all the fun you and your family can have together. But let's face it, you're going to need energy to live a more active lifestyle. Those active weekends just won't happen if you're too pooped to get off the couch. Those active vacations won't be much fun if you're in terrible physical condition and spend the whole time complaining about your aching muscles.

Although this is not a "fitness book," the issue of fitness *is important* to families who want to play together and stay together. We're not talking about fitness as an end in itself. We're talking about it as a means to an end. Believe it or not, family, fitness, and fun really can

---

*Eric Perkins, *Staying Thin for Kids* (N.Y.: Nautilis Books, 1988), p. 25.

go together. You wouldn't think so based on most fitness programs out there!

Most fitness experts promote *solo* activities, and they are just so serious all the time!! The last thing we want to see you do is sign up for some so-called fitness program that *steals precious time away from the family*. The average American apparently agrees with us. A study commissioned by Hilton Hotels revealed that the number one goal of Americans for the 1990s is to spend more time with their family and friends. That goal cannot be achieved when Dad is lifting weights with the guys, Mom is doing aerobics with the ladies, and the kids are off playing team sports with their peers. We think life is too short and families are too precious for that approach.

Our goal is to help you put the fun back into fitness, while promoting family togetherness. Sound like the impossible dream? It's not. Rather than jogging alone five mornings a week, Dad, why not take the whole family for a brisk walk after dinner each evening? Rather than signing the kids up for baseball, why not join a hiking club *as a family*? It doesn't have to be rigid. Your family can play volleyball or go to the beach or enjoy a round of table tennis or just stroll through the park. That's the kind of fitness that builds positive memories and lifelong healthy habits.

You may be thinking, "Hey, I thought getting fit was supposed to be miserable." The good news is that a lifestyle of active outdoor enjoyment has far more long-term fitness benefits than a two-year jogging binge that ends with an injury. So, how will you break the news to the kids that you plan to get fit as part of your journey to becoming an *active family*? More importantly, how can you get your children on board and excited about the possibilities? There are no magic formulas, but here are a few ideas that might just help:

- **Call a family meeting.** Didn't you watch the Brady Bunch? They always organized family meetings and it worked every time. (Of course, they also managed to resolve all conflicts within thirty minutes minus commercial time. . . .) Seriously, gather the family together one evening after dinner and say, "Listen, if we're going to become an active family, taking all these neat vacations and mini-vacations, we'd better get in shape!" It isn't the time to tell your family they're lazy, or overweight, it's a time to talk about how much you love your family, how much you enjoy spending time with them, and how much FUN you're going to have *playing together*.

Perhaps you feel the family is too sedentary. Or maybe your kids are involved in too many activities that take them away from the family. You *should* be concerned. But when you talk to the kids, focus on the positive. Focus on the benefits. Let's say the whole family is excited about a biking or hiking adventure as this year's vacation. Well, work toward the goal of *enjoying* the vacation by getting fit in advance. You'll be amazed how motivating it is to put up a poster of your upcoming adventure. By the way, we're a poster family. Even as we write, there's a giant poster of the dude ranch we're planning to visit this summer. It inspires us to take our nightly walk!

- **Tell them you love them too much to neglect their health.** When I was growing-up during the '60s and '70s, it was commonly believed that some people were blessed with good health, while others were not. It was as if "the gods" mysteriously sent down medical afflictions on innocent, unsuspecting souls without rhyme or reason. My poor mother fell victim to "the ignorance of the age." Because we didn't realize the power of lifestyle changes, she was constantly in-and-out of the hospital with everything from hemorrhages to heart attacks. We just couldn't understand why so many horrible things happened to her.

  Well, this is the 1990s and now we know better! The reality is: good health is *not* a mystery. While some people are clearly blessed with better genes, *heredity plays a minor role in our overall health*. With some exceptions, our health is largely determined by our lifestyle. Again, OUR HEALTH IS DETERMINED LARGELY BY OUR LIFESTYLE. We can choose whether or not we want to spend our lives cooped up in hospital beds. We can also decide whether or not we want to see our children end up like that.

We know you want the best for your family. You want to stay together for decades to come. So, explain to your kids that you now realize that the number one determining factor of a person's health *is the way he/she lives.* Barring some tragic event, an active lifestyle is guaranteed to prolong the lives of everyone in your family and will dramatically improve the quality of the years you spend together on this planet.

In case your kids want proof, here are the statistics about what contributes to our health:*

Medical/10 percent

Environment/16 percent

Heredity/21 percent

Lifestyle/53 percent

- **Give your whole family a sense of ownership.** If there is one thing virtually everyone resents, it is "edicts from the boss." Your children are no different. Get everyone involved and don't insist that things will be done your way or no way. If they sense that this active family lifestyle is being forced on them from above—whether they like it or not, whether they understand it or not—they will fight you with everything they've got. (And they've got a lot!) On the other hand, if you can convince your kids that *they* thought up the idea of getting fit, you're on the way to a healthier, more productive and meaningful family life. Harry Truman once said, "I have found the best way to give advice to your children is to find out what they want and then advise them to do it."

---

*Raymond and Dorothy Moore, *Homemade Health* (Word).

- **Develop a Family Wellness Profile.** The following questions will help you get a realistic handle on your current level of wellness and get you thinking about the areas where you'll need to make changes if you want the energy to live a more active lifestyle:

    1. Do you (as parents) use food as a reward?
    2. What do you usually serve for dessert?
    3. How often do you serve dessert?
    4. What do most family members drink when they are thirsty?
    5. What do you do if you (or the children) get hungry running an errand around town?
    6. When friends come from out of town to visit, what activities do you do? Do you eat out at restaurants or do you go to active places?
    7. When you visit another city, what activities do you do? Do you take a tour of the restaurant district . . . or do you go hiking?
    8. When someone reaches a goal, wins an award, or achieves some special accomplishment, how do you reward him/her?
    9. What do you usually do in the evening after dinner?
    10. Do you eat when you are bored?
    11. Do any family members smoke?
    12. Do any family members drink alcohol?
    13. Describe your last vacation (i.e., active or passive).
    14. Describe your typical vacation (i.e., active or passive).
    15. Describe your activities during a typical weekend.
    16. How often do family members eat in front of the television?
    17. Do you leave the television on during dinner or other meals?
    18. How many hours a day do you exercise?
    19. How many hours a day do you watch television?

20. Are any (or all) of your family members overweight?

- **Make it fun.** Build on the activities your children already enjoy. For example, if they love the beach, start with an active beach vacation. Perhaps, in the past, Mom and Dad napped on the beach blanket the whole time. Well, this time, don't even bring a blanket. Instead, bring a beach ball, Frisbee, volleyball, etc., and enjoy an active day at the beach. If you don't live near a beach, substitute your favorite public park and make believe the sand under the swing set is really beach-front property. The idea is to just have active fun.

- **Host a fitness competition.** Some families might get excited by some friendly competition. Prepare a chart of activities and corresponding point values. At the end of one week, the person with the most points wins the prize. Just make sure the prize isn't junk food! Alternatively, your family can set a joint goal (i.e., 500 points) and when your combined points hit the target the whole family shares in the reward.

- **Let the children plan the first event.** To get your new active family fitness program off to a positive start, invite their input. Show them that Mom and Dad are willing to try new things and that you want to do things the *whole* family can enjoy, rather than forcing your pet activity on them. If your children are old enough, you can actually let them do much of the planning. If they choose bungee jumping . . . well, try to be a good sport about it!

Therefore, I urge you, brothers, in view of God's mercy, to offer your bodies as living sacrifices, holy and pleasing to God—this is your spiritual act of worship. Do not conform any longer to the pattern of this world, but be transformed by the renewing of your mind. Then you will be able to test and approve what God's will is—his good, pleasing and perfect will.

—Romans 12:1-2

Discussion Questions

1. Discuss your reaction to the statistics on what contributes to our health. Were you surprised to discover what a huge factor lifestyle is?

2. Based on your current lifestyle, is your family building toward health or illness? Below, list all those things you currently do that promote health . . . and which promote illness.

   HEALTH   *ILLNESS*

3. Let each person discuss the long-term implications of the choices they make on a daily basis.

4. Discuss the twenty questions posed under "develop a family wellness profile" and the implications of your answers.

Suggested Family Activities

1. Invite the kids to plan the first family fitness event. Tell them Mom and Dad will do whatever they come up with.

2. Plan a family fitness competition. Decide whether to award individual prizes, work toward a group prize, or maybe a combination of both. And, of course, decide what the illustrious prizes will be.

Active Family Journal

While you're getting fit, why don't you include your parents?

—Arnold Schwarzenegger

Record your reaction to the family fitness competition.

_____
_____
_____
_____
_____
_____
_____
_____
_____
_____
_____
_____
_____
_____
_____
_____
_____
_____
_____
_____
_____
_____
_____
_____
_____
_____

INSTRUCTIONS FOR FITNESS COMPETITION

Individual Competition

Prepare a master list of activities worth 10 points (or a multiple of 10 points) each. Be sure to include time value or specific count. For example, 45-minute walk, 30-minute bike ride, 20 laps of swimming, three rounds of table tennis might all be worth 10 points. An active day at the beach could be worth 30 points while a full-day hike earns 50 points. You can decide as a family how challenging it will be to earn points. Obviously, families with young children will set more modest targets than a family with teenagers.

Post the chart in a prominent location. To complete it, write in family member names along the bottom of the chart. Then, each time someone completes a 10-point activity, they fill it in on the chart. Optional: Assign each family member a color, then lightly color each completed block. Then everyone can see at a glance who is ahead in the competition (without obstructing the information on HOW they are getting ahead!).

Family Fitness Competition

Using the instructions above, complete the list of activities. However, in order to qualify for the competition, *all family members* must complete the activity. In other words, if Dad swims 20 laps, the family doesn't earn 10 points. If the *whole family* swims 20 laps *combined*, the family earn the points. Color in the chart each time you earn 10 or more points. When you reach the top, treat your family to the predetermined reward.

Fitness Competition

Activity List

Activity	Time/Count	Points

Fitness Competition

Individual

Grand Prize:

Runner-up:

2nd Runner-up:

200					
190					
180					
170					
160					
150					
140					
130					
120					
110					
100					
90					
80					
70					
60					
50					
40					
30					
20					
10					
Name:					

Fitness Competition

Family

Family Prize:

200	
190	
180	
170	
160	
150	
140	
130	
120	
110	
100	
90	
80	
70	
60	
50	
40	
30	
20	
10	

Chapter 9

GETTING IN SHAPE FOR YOUR ACTIVE LIFESTYLE

Your capacity to say no determines your capacity to say yes to greater things.

—E. Stanley Jones

What will it take to get in shape for your active lifestyle? Do you have to quit your day job so you can train for a marathon? Not at all. Dr. Kenneth Cooper, author of the book *Aerobics* and father of the modern fitness movement, now says, "Very rigorous conditioning programs including different forms of overtraining, may actually backfire on your body" (*Antioxidant Revolution*). Furthermore, his studies at the Cooper Institute for Aerobics Research revealed that people who walk three miles (at a pace of twelve minutes per mile) "achieved ALL the fitness benefits that they would have gained if they had been jogging nine-minute miles."

Dr. Cooper warns, "Those who push themselves beyond what is necessary to enjoy the full benefits of aerobic fitness . . . may lose the very benefits for which they are striving." For maximum health, he recommends walking just two miles (fifteen minutes per mile or less) three times per week. Now that's a goal any family can easily achieve, even if it means pushing little ones in a jogging stroller. Dr. Cooper's extensive research backs his claim that this one small measure "will give you the amount of physical activity you need to maximize your health and longevity and minimize your production of destructive free radicals." We're talking about ninety minutes out of a week filled with 10,080 minutes. That doesn't sound like too much, does it?

You see, *it doesn't have to hurt to work.* And the really nice thing about walking is that just about anyone can do it. As one wiseguy once quipped: "Walking is easy. As long as the same leg isn't used twice in succession, nothing much can go wrong." If you're looking for maximum effectiveness, your family's aerobic exercise program should include:

1. Exercise for at least 30 minutes, three times per week.
2. Exercise rhythmically at a moderate pace. Walking, biking, and swimming are all excellent choices. Tennis and basketball are *not* good choices, for example, because they involve too much starting and stopping. (Which isn't to say you shouldn't play tennis and basketball, just that they won't help you aerobically.)
3. Cross-train. That means participating in a wide variety of activities. You will enjoy better overall fitness by alternately working various muscle groups. And you will also improve the chances that your new active lifestyle will be a permanent change because you'll actually be having fun!
4. Drink plenty of water before and after exercise. You've already heard this, but you should drink at least eight glasses of water each day.
5. Even more important than drinking water, you need to eat high-water content foods, like fruits and vegetables. (We'll cover that in Part III: Food.)

You will be glad to know that this is *precisely* the type of program we are advocating on the pages of this book: moderate exercise and a long-term commitment to gradual health improvement. So stick with us, and you will be well on your way to "maximizing your health and longevity."

The President's Challenge

If your family is already in good condition and would like to do something more challenging than a nightly walk, by all means, go for it. One unique idea that might just work—if your family can get excited about receiving an award from the President of the United States—is to participate in a program offered through the President's Council on Physical Fitness and Sports. The Council has published a free forty-page handbook, for kids ages six to seventeen, called "Get Fit: How to Get in Shape to Meet the President's Challenge."

The handbook explains fitness basics and includes a complete program (with illustrations) and a "challenge" in five different exercise categories. If your child scores at or above the "challenge" scores (time and distance measures), he or she will receive the Presidential Physical Fitness Award. Children who attempt all five test items but whose scores fall below the fiftieth percentile on one or more of them are still eligible to receive the Participant Award.

This is a great, affordable way to launch your family fitness program. For more information, write to:

President's Challenge
Poplars Research Center
400 E. 7th Street
Bloomington, IN 47405

The Presidential Sports Award

If your family would prefer working toward rewards for physical activities *of their own choosing* (rather than the pre-determined exercises required for the "Challenge") you can register for The Presidential Sports Award program. Each family member (age six and up) can track their progress in any one of sixty qualifying sports and earn certificates and patches for their efforts. There is no charge to register and options include:

aerobics	handball	skiing
archery	horseshoe pitching	soccer
backpacking	ice hockey	softball
badminton	ice skating	squash
baseball	jogging	swimming
basketball	lawn bowling	table tennis
baton twirling	martial arts	tennis
bicycling	racquetball	volleyball
bowling	roller skating	walking
dance	rope skipping	water exercise
figure skating	rowing	weight training
football	running	wrestling
gymnastics	sailing	

Family members can earn as many awards as they like in as many categories as they choose. To earn the award, select an activity and keep a record on the fitness log provided by the Council. When you have fulfilled the qualifying standards, you send in the log and receive your award. It includes a certificate of achievement (suitable for framing) from the President of the United States, along with a blazer patch. Most kids will think this is a really big deal . . . and it's so easy to do! For more information, write to:

Presidential Sports Award
P.O. Box 68207
Indianapolis, IN 46268

Family Fitness Award

In addition to individual awards, the Council now offers a Family Fitness Award. Family Fitness is awarded each time a minimum of one parent/guardian and one child apply to receive awards at the same time and meet the program criteria. So you can promote fitness and family togetherness at the same time. And that's what *Play Together Stay Together* is all about.

> *Whatever you do, work at it with all your heart, as working for the Lord.*
>
> —Colossians 3:23

Discussion Question

1. Discuss the five components of an effective aerobic program.

Suggested Family Activities

1. If interested, send for information on The President's Challenge and the Presidential Sports awards.

2. Develop a plan for a family fitness routine that features all five components of an effective aerobic program. Address each of the following areas in developing your plan.

   Which three days of the week will you exercise?

   What time of day can everyone make it?

   List all possible aerobic activities. Those everyone can agree on and for which you have—or can quickly obtain—all the needed equipment:

3. Plan to cross-train—that is, include a variety of activities each week. For example, biking Tuesday and Thursday after dinner,

and hiking on Saturday morning. You can follow the same schedule each week or *better yet*, plan for variety using the Exercise
Chart.

4. Complete the "One-Week Wellness Inventory" to get a more objective look at your present health.

Active Family Journal

He has half the deed done who has made a beginning.

—Horace

Record your family goals about becoming an active family.

_____

_____

_____

_____

_____

_____

_____

_____

_____

_____

_____

_____

_____

_____

_____

_____

_____

_____

_____

_____

_____

_____

_____

_____

One-Week Wellness Inventory

	Break-fast	Lunch	Dinner	Snacks	Active Activities (Time)	Inactive Activities (Time)
Sunday						
Monday						
Tuesday						
Wednesday						
Thursday						
Friday						
Saturday						

Exercise Chart

Week of: _____

	Planned Activity (record at beginning of week)	Actual Activity (Record actual activity & duration as completed)	Comments (who participated, milestones, etc.)
Sunday			
Monday			
Tuesday			
Wednesday			
Thursday			
Friday			
Saturday			

Chapter 10

BATTLING THE ACTIVE FAMILY'S #1 ENEMY

It is not too much to say that "habit is ten natures." We have lost sight of the fact that habit is to life what rails are to transport cars. It follows that lines of habit must be laid down toward given ends and after careful survey, or the joltings and delays of life become insupportable. More, habit is inevitable. If we fail to ease life by laying down habits of right thinking and right acting, habits of wrong thinking and wrong acting fix themselves of their own accord.

—Charlotte Mason, *A Philosophy of Education*, 1925

Are you a couch potato? Are you stuck in a rut that leads you on a direct pathway from the dinner table to the couch? Does your living room carpet have a well worn path leading to the TV set? We know how you feel because we've spent most of our lives as couch potatoes. But when you boil it down (get the joke?), staring at the tube is nothing more than a bad habit. Actually, for some people and some families, it's more like an addiction. And once you've fallen into the tube's clutches, it's hard to break away. But it can be done, and we promise the rewards will far outweigh the pain of withdrawal. Just as you have gotten into the habit of being inactive, you can get into the habit of being active. It will take a few months, but it will happen. You'll see!

We live in a planned community in Arizona called Red Mountain Ranch. Every year they have a huge yard sale with dozens of families participating. And every year as we take a tour of the goodies, we notice the same thing: the most-frequently-sighted items are *always* of the home fitness variety. People are selling off everything from stationary bikes and treadmills to weight-lifting equipment and other "can't live without it" exercise gear sold through television infomercials. Interestingly enough, one thing we have NEVER seen on sale is a television set.

What's truly sad, however, is that we are raising a generation of couch potato kids. According to research conducted by Dr. Charles T. Kuntzleman, author of *Family Fitness Fun*, on 24,000 children in Jackson County, Michigan, 96 percent of a seven- to twelve-year-old child's time is spent doing sedentary or mild activities. In contrast, only ten minutes of a child's day is devoted to appropriate levels of exercise. "By the time kids finish high school, their pattern of physical activity is set for life," says Gregory Heath, D.Sc., an epidemiologist and exercise physiologist at the Centers for Disease Control and Prevention (CDC) in Atlanta. "So it is very important to establish good habits when they're young." Unfortunately, very few families are promoting something other than couch potato-ism.

At an American Heart Association meeting, a California researcher reported too much television watching during childhood may be setting the stage for heart disease later in life. "The cholesterol levels and viewing habits of 1,066 children and adolescents age two to twenty were studied, and watching two or more hours of television daily turned out to be a stronger predictor of elevated cholesterol than any other factor."[*]

---

[*]Michael Franzone, "Kids Get Hyped," *American Fitness* (July/Aug. 1993), p. 48.

Problems With Television

When you stop to think about it, TV is a problem for three basic reasons:

1. *You almost always watch it sitting down.* How many of you have strategically placed exercise equipment near the TV and vowed to exercise while you watched? The Partows have done it! Now for the real question: How many of you *actually kept up with a consistent program of exercising while you watch?* We didn't.

2. *Most people snack mindlessly while watching.* Although scientists cannot explain it, there is apparently some mysterious connection between watching TV and the need to keep your mouth in constant motion. If a famine ever strikes America, we know where to go for crumbs—straight for the couch! We could probably feed an entire Third World nation on the crumbs gathered from the couches of America. (And in case you don't know this yet, snacking is terrible for your body.)

3. *The commercials are never for fruit.* Have you ever noticed that? Can you think of one slogan, one catchy jingle for fruit (besides Fruit of the Loom)? Instead, you are bombarded with slick advertisements promoting foods that destroy your body and mind. If you think these commercials don't affect you or your children, you might stop to consider why corporations spend *billions* of dollars putting them on the air. As a former advertising executive, I can assure you that junk food commercials would stop tomorrow if they didn't work. They do . . . and we have the most overweight nation in the history of the world to prove it.

If you ask the average family member why they don't lead a more active lifestyle, chances are the response will be: "I don't have the time." But the simple truth is, we do. Depending upon which survey you believe, the average American watches anywhere from twenty-one to thirty-five hours of TV each week. Doesn't that sound like enough time for some active family fun? It's not that we don't *have* the time, it's just that we don't *take* the time.

Will you resolve to change? As a family, will you decide to help one another fight the battle against couch potato-ism?

> *Go to the ant, you sluggard; consider its ways and be wise! It has no commander, no overseer or ruler, yet it stores its provisions in summer and gathers its food at harvest. How long will you lie there, you sluggard? When will you get up from your sleep? A little sleep, a little slumber, a little folding of the hands to rest—and poverty will come on you like a bandit and scarcity like an armed man.*
>
> —Proverbs 6:6-11

Discussion Questions

1. Discuss your family's current TV viewing habits.

2. Discuss some of the good things you are missing out on by spending your life on the couch.

3. Invite everyone to suggest how many hours per day or per week they feel is "ideal." You can set individual or family goals, if you like.

4. Let each family member who feels the need, "confess" to being a couch potato. If someone needs to have a mirror of truth held before him by the rest of the family, do it gently . . . but do it!

5. Discuss changes you plan to make in your TV viewing habits. You might even discuss the possibility of throwing out the TV or at least putting it away for a trial period (one week, one month, etc.). The intensity of the reaction will be a direct measure of the intensity of your addiction. Unless, of course, it would mean missing an NFL football game. Who could go that far?

Suggested Family Activities

1. Reproduce the chart on the following page and post it by the television set. For several weeks, keep an honest account of your viewing habits.

2. With great fanfare, move the TV to the garage or attic. Try to survive without it for a predetermined amount of time.

3. Sell your TV.

Active Family Journal

If it weren't for the fact that the TV set and the refrigerator are so far apart, some of us wouldn't get any exercise at all.

—Joey Adams, comedian

Record your reaction to the TV viewing activity you chose—whether it was monitoring your viewing or putting it away for a period of time.

TV Viewing Log

"Kick the Habit!"

Start time	Who's watching	Show	Stop time	Comments on value

Chapter 11

ACTIVE FAMILY SPORTS

Do you not know that in a race all the runners run, but only one gets the prize? Run in such a way as to get the prize. Everyone who competes in the games goes into strict training. They do it to get a crown that will not last; but we do it to get a crown that will last forever. Therefore I do not run like a man running aimlessly; I do not fight like a man beating the air. No, I beat my body and make it my slave so that after I have preached to others, I myself will not be disqualified for the prize.

—1 Corinthians 9:24–27

In previous chapters, we talked about the fun your family could have engaging in *special activities*—from a family fitness competition to tourist weekends and dude ranch vacations. But there's something to be said for *ongoing* involvement with active sports. Such a regular commitment can have an incredibly positive impact on your family. Nancy Nemitz, mother of four, reports that her thirteen-year-old daughter Sarah had been enrolled in ballet for a number of years and attended lessons twice a week. Even though ballet involved physical movement, it was a very quiet activity with little interaction with others (and, more to the point, it took her away from the family). Nancy decided to enroll her for the local swim team and the results have been excellent. Nancy recalls:

> I noticed a difference right away when we enrolled her in daily swimming. She seemed much happier. As a bonus, I was able to enroll my two younger children in swimming, so now three of them attend. And it's nice to see the kids heading in the same direction.
>
> Another advantage is that the pool is close by. We used to have to drive to ballet, but now all three of them are able to actually ride their bikes and that's much better for the family: Mom and Dad don't have to drive around town. Our whole family has caught the excitement and we swim for at least two hours a day. It makes a big difference in our family life.
>
> Sarah was always complaining about not having enough energy. With the swimming, she has so much more energy. She told me the other day she wants to start swimming on Saturday and Sunday because even she noticed that on the days she swims, she just feels better.

On the other hand, you can go too far, notes Roger Barkin, M.D., a pediatrician and author of *The Father's Guide: Raising a Healthy Child* (Fulcrum). "If you're taking your eighteen-month-old swimming at the Y or tumbling at Gymboree because you like the idea of forty-five minutes of horsing around with your little one, that's great! But if you're doing it because in the back of your mind you have visions of a future Mark Spitz or Mary Lou Retton, slow down."[*]

Before selecting any of the sports described in this chapter, be sure it's something your children want to do (or are at least willing to try). And as your involvement increases, remember the whole idea is to *play together, stay together,* and *have fun.* If you miss out on any one of those components, you're missing the point entirely.

---

[*]Herman Hank, "Playing Together," *Ladies' Home Journal* (June 1991), p. 84.

This chapter provides you with a brief introduction to some of the more popular sports your family can enjoy together. Admittedly, some of them are geared toward families with older children, but never fear, you can take a *baby* biking or hiking. Besides, if there's one thing you can be sure about, it's that your children will get a little older every day. Maybe you can't cross-country ski this year, but give it a year or two and you'll be trying to keep up with the kids. For now, choose whatever suits your family in terms of ages and abilities.

As you begin considering which sport(s) might be ideal for your family, be sure to factor in the following:

- **Where you live.** Your location should immediately suggest the types of activities that might be right for you. If your home is thirty minutes from the beach, consider water sports. If you live near the mountains, what about hiking or skiing? Of course, it's possible to live within miles of a nationally acclaimed ski resort . . . and still have no interest in skiing. Nevertheless, looking at the activities that are most readily available is a good place to start.

- **Climate.** Do you live in the hot, sunny desert? Or the wet Northwest? Is the temperature moderate year round or do you experience dramatic weather patterns as the seasons change? That will affect the type and variety of activities you can plan.

- **Ages.** Do you have three teenagers? Or three preschoolers? You'll need to factor in the ages of your children as you plan. That can be tough. We know: We have a teenager, a six-year-old, and a newborn.

- **Level of fitness.** Make an honest evaluation of your family's current fitness level, using the resources listed in the previous chapter. Trying to climb a mountain when you can barely climb out of bed is not wise. If you are a couch-potato family, plan to start slow and build up over time.

Remember the moral we learned from "The Tortoise and the Hare": slow and steady beats rapid burnout, every time.

- **Number of family members.** Some activities work better with small groups, others require a crowd. It's tough to play softball with Mom, Dad, and a toddler, but Mom, Dad, and eight kids can sure make a game of it. Canoeing is great for a family of three . . . but how about a family of ten? That's an awful lot of canoes to keep track of, not to mention the expense. Come to think of it, let's mention the expense. . . .

- **Budget.** Now, about those canoes for ten people—it's something to think about before you undertake any activity. What's your budget for active family fun? Is it even *in* your budget? If not, where can you cut back to allow funds for activities. If becoming an active family is going to become a reality, it's going to cost you some money. On the other hand, don't go overboard. A few trips to the ski shop or sporting goods store can set you back in a hurry. Don't rush out and spend money until you've determined your long-term commitment. Set realistic spending goals and stay within those limits.

- **Time.** Does Dad work seventy hours a week? That doesn't leave much time for family fun. Dad should reconsider his priorities and cut back that work schedule. If he can't, then you'll have to focus on the quality rather than quantity of activities. Also take a look at the children's schedules. Do they need to cut back on outside activities? What if Mom and Dad both work? What if yours is a single-parent home? Is there still time for playing together? Yes, but only if you schedule the time and remain committed to becoming an active family.

- **Experience.** What do you have to build on? Our neighbors Werner and Elissa Wolf both came from "camping families" and grew up with a wealth of outdoor experiences. Cameron's family thought "the great outdoors" was what you walked through to get from the house to the chauffeur-driven car. Donna grew up playing outdoors, but had only participated in very unstructured, informal activities. Obviously, the Wolfs and Partows need to take very different approaches to active family life. The Wolfs can head off into the wilderness, while we need to stick to the beaten path—preferably with a tour guide. Evaluate your experience, then get started right where you are.

Canoeing, Rowing, and Kayaking

Equipment Needed

- ☐ Body of Water
- ☐ Canoe, Rowboat, or Kayak
- ☐ Life Vests

Unless you live in a very mild climate with convenient access to water, these sports will probably serve as only occasional fun. In that case, stick with renting the equipment you need. However, if you decide your family will be on the water often enough to justify the investment, check out the classified ads. Our friends the Martineaus are definitely "a canoeing family." They bought an almost-new canoe for $400, and it was worth every penny to them. Since they live in Arizona quite close to several man-made lakes, they use their canoe virtually year-round.

How To

As always, a lesson or two is a wise investment. If that's not possible, Human Kinetics has published an excellent book, *Canoeing*, by Laurie Gullion, as well as an instructional video (call 800-747-4457). We know you don't feel like reading a book or watching a video. You want to dip those oars into the water and get started.

But you won't have much fun if you spend the whole day tipping over. Believe us, we *know*. So, get lessons or get the book! Maintaining balance and developing a smooth stroke are the two keys to successfully navigating the water. Speaking of water, choose a calm, predictable body of water when you're just starting out. If your choices are (1) going into turbulent water or (2) loading the kids back into the car and heading home *with no adventure* under your hats, please choose option 2—*turn around*. Even very moderate turbulence can throw you overboard. Once again, this is the voice of experience speaking.

Resources

Books:

Bennett, Jeff. *The Complete Whitewater Rafter* (Ragged Mountain Press).

Gullion, Laurie. *Canoeing* (Human Kinetics Publishers). 800-747-4457

Magazines/Catalogs:

American Whitewater Affiliate Magazine
P.O. Box 85
Phoenicia, NY 12464

Canoe & Kayak Magazine
10526 NE 68th
P.O. Box 3146
Kirkland, WA 98083
800-678-5432

Organizations:

American Canoe Association
7432 Alban Station Blvd.
Suite B-226

Springfield, VA 22150
703-451-0141

Cross-Country Skiing

Cross-country skiing is safe and easy to learn, and you can get the whole family involved, from preschoolers on up. It's one of the absolute best all-around workouts, involving every part of your body. On the downside, of course, your *whole body* will feel it. Unlike most aerobic exercises, cross-country skiing relies on gentle, gliding motions. Since most injuries result from sudden jarring motions, cross-country skiing is a very safe bet.

Equipment needed

- [ ] Warm, layered clothing (head-to-toe underwear is important. It pulls perspiration away from your skin to keep you warm and dry).
- [ ] Skis
- [ ] Bindings
- [ ] Boots
- [ ] Warm cap
- [ ] Socks
- [ ] Gloves
- [ ] Sunglasses
- [ ] Sunscreen lotion
- [ ] Poles with wrist straps (should be at least as long as the distance from the ground to your armpit)

How To

If you have never tried cross-country skiing, ideally you should learn from a qualified instructor. Most ski resorts offer instructions, along with equipment rentals. As a beginner, the most important thing is to look out for the *hills*. If you can't avoid hills, don't attempt to ski down. Take your skis off and walk down.

Once your family gets the hang of cross-country skiing (and you find out about those muscles you didn't know you had), you might enjoy taking a cross-country ski tour, such as those offered by Backroads (800-GO-ACTIVE). It makes a great fitness vacation for the whole family.

Resources

Books:

Caldwell, John. *The Cross-Country Ski Book*. Viking/Penguin.
Dostal, John, and Ned Gillette. 1984. *Cross-Country Skiing*. Bantam.

Instructional Video:

Cross-Country Skiing with Jeff Nowak
Sybervision
Fountain Square
6066 Civic Terrace Ave.
Newark, CA 94560
800-255-9666

Magazines/Catalogs:

Cross Country Skier
1823 Fremont Ave. S.
Minneapolis, MN 55403

Eagle River Nordic
P.O. Box 936
Eagle River, WI 54521
800-423-9730

New Moon Ski-Shop
P.O. Box 132
Hayward, WI 54843
715-634-8685

Organizations:

Ski Touring Council
West Hill Road
Troy, VT 05868
Promotes noncompetitive cross-country skiing and touring

Cycling

If we were to replace cars with bicycles, we'd all be better off. It would be better for our cardiovascular system, our disposition, and certainly our finances. As recreation, cycling takes you further faster than virtually any other sport. Your whole family can enjoy beautiful scenery while benefiting from an aerobic workout that's far less jarring than running or even walking. Once again, teenagers and most adolescents should be able to keep pace or surpass Mom and Dad. The little ones can ride comfortably in a bike trailer. For adults, the ideal cycling speed is fifteen miles per hour. Any slower than that yields minimal aerobic benefit; faster than that puts you at a racer's clip. Remember: you're not in a hurry, you're trying to have fun playing with your family.

Equipment Needed

- ☐ Helmet (tell your kids it's a "skid-lid" and they'll think it's cool).
- ☐ Bike
- ☐ Gloves
- ☐ Loud horn
- ☐ Rack or saddlebag
- ☐ Water-bottle cage

If your family is new at this active family game and you are not sure cycling will be right for you, you can get started with borrowed or second-hand bikes. Check out yard sales for adult bikes and your friends' garages for kids' bikes. Since kids' bikes come in all shapes and sizes, you may actually be doing them a great favor by clearing out last year's models. We've noticed that second-hand bikes are very easy to come by—which should make you think twice about spending a small fortune on new bikes. Obviously, lots of people who invest in bikes soon find it's not the right sport for them. Next thing you know, their bikes are gathering dust in the garage, and it's only a matter of time before they get tagged "For Sale, $20." Don't make the same mistake.

If, after three months or so, you are convinced yours is "a cycling family," it's time to buy the *right* bikes. Choosing the right bike is neither easy nor cheap. The right bike depends on what type of terrain you'll be covering: streets, dirt roads, mountain passes. Another factor is intensity: are you looking for a serious workout or leisurely Sunday afternoon rides? There are touring bikes, recreational-sport bikes, and mountain bikes, to name a few. Prices range from $100 for your basic, run-of-the-mill bike to $4,000 for a super-deluxe mountain bike.

The bicycle frame should be proportionate to your height and leg length. When you sit down, both feet should just barely touch the ground, and your leg should be slightly bent when your foot reaches the bottom of pedaling movement. Speaking of sitting—be sure the seat fits your body comfortably. Then pad it with a sheepskin or chamois seat cover.

The next thing to consider is riding position. No doubt you've seen spandex-covered cyclists zooming along the road hunched over in a racer's crouch. If you intend to race, the aerodynamic design of dropped handles is the only choice. For the rest of us mere mortals, upright handlebars make more sense. They are much easier on the posture and enable you to enjoy the view and the ride (not to mention keeping an eye on your kids).

The next consideration is tire width. Once again, don't assume you need to follow the racer's lead by selecting a skinny tire. A wide tire grips the road more securely, preventing falls, which is especially important if you'll be covering different types of terrain. Plus, wider tires are better "shock absorbers" and provide a smoother ride.

Although mountain bikes are more expensive than traditional

ten-speed bikes, they have all the right ingredients for "Play To-gether, Stay Together": upright handlebars, wide tires, and com-fortable seats. Of course, be sure you test drive any bike before put-ting your money down.

How To

As you probably guessed from the previous section, the most important "how to" is selecting the right bike. Next, the whole fam-ily should take a short course in bicycle safety (see resources). Once you've done that, hop on and ride.

Cycling (Mountain Biking)

Equipment Needed

- ☐ Mountain Bike
- ☐ Helmet
- ☐ Water bottle
- ☐ Lightweight, tight-fitting clothing (baggy pants can catch in the chain)
- ☐ In cold weather, fleece or wool tops and synthetic pants
- ☐ First-aid kit

How To

Mountain bikes are very expensive, but can be rented afforda-bly. Many ski resorts convert to mountain bike lodges after the snow melts and the mud hardens. Before hitting the slopes . . . that is, trails, be sure to ask,

- • Is the terrain safe for children?
- • What age should they be?
- • Are instructions available?
- • How old are the bikes?
- • How often are the bikes serviced?
- • Do they offer half-day programs?
- • Are tour guides available?

Resources

Books:

Davis, Don, and Dave Carter. *Mountain Biking.*
Human Kinetics Press. 800-747-4457.

Oliver, Peter. *Touring and Mountain Bike Basics.* W. W. Norton.

Magazines/Catalogs:

American Bicyclist
400 Skokie Blvd. #395
Northbrook, IL 60062

Bicycling Magazine
33 East Minor St.
Emmaus, PA 18098

Bike
33046 Calle Aviador,
P.O. Box 1028
San Juan Capistrano, CA 92675
800-289-0636

Cycle World
853 West 17th
Costa Mesa, CA 92627

Outside Magazine
Box 54729
Boulder, CO 80322
800-678-1131

Organizations:

Bicycle USA
League of American Wheelmen

Suite 209
6707 Whitestone Rd.
Baltimore, MD 21207

The Consumer Product Safety Commission
Washington, DC 20207
   Offers fact sheet #10 on bicycle safety, selection, and main-
tenance

Fitness Walking

Equipment Needed

☐ Your Feet
☐ Good walking shoes

How To

   More than two hundred years ago, Thomas Jefferson said,
"Walking is the best exercise. Habituate yourself to walk very far."
We think that's excellent advice. Your technique should include
long, swift strides and a full-arm swing. If your walking route includes hills—especially a long, slow incline—all the better. With
the addition of hand-held weights and an exaggerated swing, the
sport is considered power walking. Start with half a pound to two
pounds, depending upon your level of upper-body strength and
overall fitness. I have also tried wearing ankle weights, but was cau-
tioned that it's not wise to do so. They cause undo stress to the knee
and ankle joints, which can result in injury.
   Depending upon your fitness goals, the following chart gives
you an idea of how quickly you should be walking. I aim for a thir-
teen-minute mile, midway between fitness and race walking. Our
just-turned-teenager, Nikki, can usually keep up with Mom, which
is much more than we can say for Cameron! You can even bring the
little ones fitness walking. Just put them in a jogging stroller and
voila! You're keeping the family together and building upper-body
strength at the same time.

Speed	Time per mile
Moderate	20 minutes
Fitness Walking	15 minutes
Race Walking	12 minutes

Resources

Books:

Fletcher, Colin. *The Complete Walker III.* Knopf.

Ikonian, Therese. *Fitness Walking.* Human Kinetics Press. 800-747-4457.

Rudner, Ruth. *Walking.* Human Kinetics Press. 800-747-4457.

Magazines/Catalogs:

The Walkers Magazine
711 Boylston St.
Boston, MA 02116

Organizations:

The Walkers Club of America
445 E. 86th St.
New York, NY 10028

Hiking/Backpacking

Equipment Needed
☐ Your feet
☐ Hiking shoes (preferably hiking boots for ankle support)
☐ Backpack
☐ Sturdy walking stick

How To

To hike is "to go on an extended walk for pleasure or exercise. So hiking is simply a term for a specialized kind of walking. And backpacking means taking a hike carrying everything you need to stay out overnight" (*Hiking and Backpacking*). The most important consideration is getting the right equipment and topping the list is first-quality hiking books.

If your family has never tried hiking before, one way to get started is by taking short, guided hikes at state or national parks. When you are ready to graduate to longer trips—maybe even overnight—your best bet is joining forces with experienced hikers. Whether it's a neighboring family or a formal hiking organization, you'll feel more at ease knowing you have knowledgeable hikers on the trail with you. Besides, hiking is more fun with a group.

There are now a variety of companies that offer hiking vacations, such as Backroads (800-GO-ACTIVE) and Country Walkers (800-464-9255). They provide experienced guides, meals, lodging, or tents. And best of all, there's usually a van to carry the heavier gear . . . including *you* if you run out of steam. Also, you can rent the necessary backpacking equipment. (As always, don't rush out and *buy* backpacking gear until you are sure your family plans to stick with it.)

Two resources that are especially worthwhile are *Backpacking With Babies and Small Children*, and *The Backpacker's Handbook*. Both can be ordered from the Adventurous Traveler Bookstore at 800-282-3963.

Backpacking With Babies and Small Children features the collected wisdom of backpacking parents with a variety of experiences in dealing with clothing, food, and equipment, all with the aim of keeping the little ones happy, healthy, and safe. *The Backpacker's Handbook* is considered the most thorough guide available on the fundamentals of backpacking. Quite current, the handbook covers the latest gear, cooking techniques, skills, and environmental hazards all with an emphasis on minimizing impact and enjoying the outdoors to the fullest extent possible. Whether you're new to backpacking or an "old pro," this book will be both enlightening and highly educational.

Resources

Books:

Manning, Harvey. *Backpacking: One Step at a Time*. Vintage Books.

Seaborg, Eric, and Ellen Dudley. *Hiking and Backpacking*. Human Kinetics. 800-747-4457.

Silverman, Goldie. *Backpacking With Babies and Small Children*. Wilderness Press. 800-282-3963.

Townsend, Chris. *Backpacker's Handbook*. McGraw Hill. 800-282-3963.

Magazines/Catalogs:

American Hiker
P.O. Box 20160
Washington, D.C. 20041

Backpacker
33 E. Minor Street
Emmaus, PA 18098
800-666-3434

Organizations:

American Hiking Society
P.O. Box 20160
Washington, D.C. 20041
703-255-9304

In-Line Skating

Equipment Needed

☐ In-line skates
☐ Helmet
☐ Knee and arm pads

How To

In-line skating burns fat, increases aerobic capacity, and reduces stress as effectively as running, but with less stress to the joints, and as effectively as cycling, for a lot less money. For a truly aerobic workout, it is important to keep skating continuously so that your legs and arms are in constant motion; coasting is fun, but it won't do your heart much good. Not that having fun isn't *enough*, but we thought we'd throw in that disclaimer about the aerobic workout in case some family out there is planning to build their entire fitness program around In-line skating. You can do it, but you've got to keep rolling.

When choosing In-line skates, don't settle for the low-end. Look for good boots that are high enough to support your ankles and that have a well-padded tongue. Be sure the boots fit well at the anklebones, arches, toes, heels, and Achilles tendons, otherwise you will be setting yourself up for injury, and that's definitely *no fun*!

Resources

Magazines/Mail-Order Catalogs:

Eagle River Nordic
P.O. Box 936
Eagle River, WI 54521
800-423-9730

New Moon Ski Shop
P.O. Box 132
Hayward, WI 54843
715-643-8685

North American Sports Training
9700 W. 76th St.
Suite T
Minneapolis, MN 55344
800-328-0171

Swimming

Equipment Needed

☐ Body of water: pool, lake, pond, river, ocean
☐ Swimsuit
☐ Goggles

How To

Swimming is the second most popular sport in America (after walking). It provides a wonderful aerobic workout for the whole body, exercising the shoulders, arms, chest, back, hips, and legs. And because the water provides all-over muscle support, it helps prevent injuries to bones, muscles, and joints. Swimming is reinvigorating, rather than exhausting or physically draining.

Again, if your family feels swimming can become a central component of your active lifestyle, investing in lessons may be in order. If that's not possible, remember the key to good swimming form is to float high and flat in the water and to use rhythmic, not erratic, strokes. Try to stay parallel to the surface and distribute your weight evenly.

Other water sports include hydro-walking, hydro-running, and water aerobics. All provide excellent workouts without putting undo stress on your joints. The older you are, the more you understand how important that is.

Resources

Books:

Elder, Terri. *Water Fun and Fitness*. Human Kinetics Press. 800-747-4457.

Magazines/Catalogs:

Aquatics

6255 Barfield Rd.
Atlanta, GA 30328-4318
Editorial: 404-256-9800

Swimming World
P.O. Box 45497
Los Angeles, CA 90045

Choose Your Own Sport

Well, those are just a few of the more popular family-oriented sports to consider. There are literally hundreds more, so if none of the ideas described here strikes your fancy, then strike out on your own. If you'd like some inspiration as you seek to discover a fun family sport, check out the Human Kinetics catalog. Their books are not only wonderfully written and informative, without being boring, they are beautiful to behold with full-color photos that virtually beg you to explore the great outdoors. We are really impressed with this publisher. Call 747-4457 to obtain a free catalog. Look it over, then get up and get going!

No discipline seems pleasant at the time, but painful. Later on, however, it produces a harvest of righteousness and peace for those who have been trained by it. Therefore, strengthen your feeble arms and weak knees.
—Hebrews 12:11-12

Discussion Question

1. Discuss which of the sports listed you would like to investigate further.

Suggested Family Activities

1. Check your local library for books and magazines on your chosen sport.

2. Call the 800 numbers or send away for other resources listed.

Active Family Journal

Do you not know that your body is a temple of the Holy Spirit, who is in you, whom you have received from God? Your are not your own; you were bought at a price. Therefore honor God with your body.

—1 Corinthians 6:19-20

Record your progress in investigating your chosen sport.

_____

_____

_____

_____

_____

_____

_____

_____

_____

_____

_____

_____

_____

_____

_____

_____

_____

_____

_____

_____

_____

_____

_____

_____

THE FAMILY THAT PLAYS TOGETHER NEEDS TO EAT RIGHT

What a grown person likes to eat or drink depends largely on what that person was trained to eat or drink as a child. And a child can be trained to like almost any sort of food or drink, either good or bad. No small responsibility, therefore, for both the health and the enjoyment of a child, devolves on him who has in hand the training of a child's appetite.... When a mother says, "My boy won't eat potatoes," or, "He won't eat tomatoes," or, "He will eat no meat but beef," she simply confesses to her culpable failure of duty in the training of her boy's appetite.... And in that answer the mother shows that all the blame in the case rests on herself, and not on her [child]. [Her child] ought to have been trained to eat what is good for him, instead of indulging his personal whims in the eating line.

—H. Clay Trumbell, nineteenth-century author

Chapter 12

WHY FAMILIES THAT PLAY TOGETHER NEED TO EAT RIGHT

"When you sit to dine, note well what is before you, and put a knife to your throat if you are given to gluttony."

—Proverbs 23:1-2

As people who would choose potato chips and oreo cookies over a banana any day of the week, we know how hard it is to change eating habits. And we know it's even tougher to change the eating habits of your kids. Nevertheless, an active lifestyle requires fuel. And that means some dietary modifications are in order. It'll be tough, but it can be done. And if it makes you feel any better, parents have been struggling to get their kids to eat right for at least a hundred years. Look what Clay Trumbell wrote in 1890:

> A child can be trained to like whatever he ought to eat, and to refrain from the eating of whatever is not best for him. And herein is the principle of wise training in the realm of a child's appetite.
>
> A prominent American educator put this principle into practice in his own family, consisting of four boys and four

girls. He was a man of limited means, and he felt the necessity of training his children to eat such food as he deemed proper for them, and as good as he could afford to supply. His choice of food for his family table was wisely made, to begin with, and then he showed wisdom in his mode of pressing it upon his children.

If those children deemed a dish distasteful, they were privileged to wait until they were willing to eat it. There was no undue pressure brought to bear on them. They could simply eat it, or let it alone. If they went without it that meal, the same dish, or a similar one, was before them for the next meal and so on until hunger gave them the zest to eat it with unfeigned heartiness. By this means those children learned to eat what they ought to eat; and when they had come to years of maturity they realized the value of this training, which had made them the rulers of their appetite, instead of being its slaves. . . . It is for the parents to decide, with the help of a good medical counsel, what their children ought to like, and then to train them to like it.

—*Hints on Child Training*, by H. Clay Trumbell (reprinted by Great Expectations Books, selected excerpts from pages 64-67).

What Should Your Kids be Eating?

No doubt you have heard about the all-new "food pyramid." What you may NOT have heard is that it was developed by a committee of bureaucrats and special interest groups with everything *except* your family's health in mind. Hold on to your seat, because we're about to expose the negative effect many of the recommended foods actually have on your family.

Fats, Oils, and Sweets

Do Americans really need to be reminded to consume fats, oils, and sweets? Be serious! We do enough of that on our own, thank you very much. (Well, the Partows do, anyway!) Unless you have been living on another planet for the past decade, you know that fat in

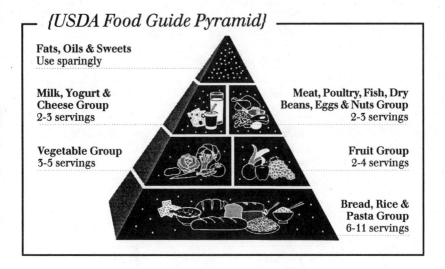

{USDA Food Guide Pyramid}

Fats, Oils & Sweets
Use sparingly

Milk, Yogurt &
Cheese Group
2-3 servings

Meat, Poultry, Fish, Dry
Beans, Eggs & Nuts Group
2-3 servings

Vegetable Group
3-5 servings

Fruit Group
2-4 servings

Bread, Rice &
Pasta Group
6-11 servings

your diet is a major contributor to virtually all of the degenerative diseases plaguing this country.

It is a proven fact that fat causes fat. And obesity is a significant indicator for many health problems including heart attacks and diabetes. Besides, you're gonna have a tough time playing together if your family is overweight. (By the way, we've observed that weight problems usually run in families, although there are obvious exceptions. That is to say, overweight parents frequently have overweight children and vice versa.)

In less-well-informed days, people who wanted to watch their weight counted calories. It didn't work. That's because *calories* are wonderful! They are the fuel that drives your body. Calories do not make you fat. FAT calories make you fat.

The following chart illustrates the HUGE volume of healthy

food you can consume versus minuscule amounts of junk food—
and walk away with the same number of fat grams. Eating healthy
doesn't mean starving yourself. It means eating foods that fuel your
body rather than drag you down.

Fat Grams			
6	1 chocolate chip cookie	800 grapes	6 cups pasta
8	1 oz. American cheese	60 carrots	12 cups pineapple
10	1 Hershey Bar	50 cups eggplant	35 cups popcorn
13	1 Snickers bar	30 cups green peppers	42 cups rice
23	1 cup granola	125 cups zucchini	150 oranges
30	1 cheeseburger	80 cups broccoli	50 apples
60	12 oz. T-bone steak	150 cups green beans	50 English muffins
75	3 cheese enchiladas	70 cups navy beans	100 bagels

We love sugar as much as the next guy. And when Nikki makes
her legendary Snickerdoodles, Mom devours half of them. But John
Yudkin, Physician Biochemist and Emeritus Professor of Nutrition
at London University (*Healthy Habits*), says, "If only a fraction of
what is already known about the effects of sugar were to be revealed in relation to any other material used as a food additive, that
material would promptly be banned." In spite of this, the average
American eats 100–150 pounds of sugar per year. "Researchers
have recently found that substantial sugar intake—especially [when
combined] with cholesterol and saturated fat—increases the serum
triglyceride levels of the blood, a condition which may be as con-
ducive to heart disease as abnormally high cholesterol. Few realize
that sugar is also rapidly converted in the liver to fat (triglycerides)
which is still another factor in heart disease and obesity" (*Homemade Health*).

Sugar is a negative food. Sugar "offers empty calories because important vitamins and minerals are stripped away during the refining process. Nevertheless, in order to be metabolized and properly absorbed into the body, it must have these minerals. So sugar robs the body of nutrients, having a devastating effect on our emotions, behavior, and mental health" (*Homemade Health*). Let's make it simple: avoid sugar wherever you can. We know it's hard, and we haven't succeeded entirely, but we *do* try. We've found an alternative called fructose. It is a fruit-derived sugar, available at health food stores.

Milk, Yogurt, and Cheese Group

God made cow's milk to be just right . . . for baby cows. So if you happen to be a baby cow, we urge you to drink as much of it as you possibly can. However, if you are *not* a baby cow, why are you drinking cow's milk?

Not only is cow's milk *filled* with artificial hormones, pesticides from the grain, and other dangerous chemicals and additives, it is one of the worst potential troublemakers in terms of behavioral problems and irritability. According to nutritional experts David and Anne Frahm, dairy products are linked to gastrointestinal problems like canker sores, vomiting, colic, colitis, diarrhea, and constipation; respiratory problems including hay fever, asthma, bronchitis, sinusitis, colds, runny noses, and ear infections and (as we've already seen) behavioral problems including irritability, restlessness, hyperactivity, headaches (including migraines), lethargy, fatigue, muscle pain, mental depression, and bed wetting (*Healthy Habits*). Enough said?

Again, we know this is tough to do! And the truth is, we ordered Pizza Hut last Friday night. However, any progress you can make toward cutting back on dairy (cow's milk, cheese, cream, ice cream, yogurt, and butter) will benefit your health. It may even result in substantially improved mood and behavior. You can substitute soy milk, rice milk, and nut milks instead.

When people discover that cow's milk may not be good for

them, their first concern is calcium. "Where will we get our calcium?" they cry. Well, adult cows don't drink milk, and they produce lots of calcium. Where do cows get calcium? From vegetables . . . and that's where we should get it, too.

Meat, Poultry, Fish, Dry Beans, Eggs, and Nuts Group

As Americans, we tend to think of a meal as "meat and . . .": meat and vegetables, meat and potatoes, meat and pasta. If you want to experience maximum vitality as you *play together*, and you want everyone in your family healthy so you can *stay together* for many years to come, you've got to shift your thinking about meat. "A high-animal-protein diet, especially an excess of meat, is definitely detrimental to the health and may be a contributor to or a direct cause of the development of many of our most common diseases, as shown by recent massive research," according to Paavo Airola, Ph.D, author of *The Airola Diet and Cookbook* (quoted in *Healthy Habits*, by David and Anne Frahm).

Meat should *not* play an important role in your diet. We believe that, ideally, you should eat a vegetarian diet, although we ourselves do not follow a strict vegetarian diet. The second best choice, which we have done, is to eliminate all red meat and stick to fish and poultry. Now you may be wondering, "Where will we get our protein?" The good news is you can get plenty of protein from beans and nuts *without* cholesterol or saturated fats. And we promise, by eliminating red meat, you'll have much more energy for playing together. Of course, if you have a cookout with burgers and hot dogs once in a while, you'll probably live to tell about it. You can even find Cameron at the grill, flipping the occasional burger.

Fruit Group

Now we're talking! Fruit is great, especially if you are able to produce your own. We'll have a lot more to say about fruit in the next chapter, so for now, just remember: an apple a day is a great idea.

If you're looking for some energy to play with in the meantime, eat a banana or an orange—the top two fruit fuels.

Vegetable Group

It's virtually impossible to consume too many vegetables. If you get in the habit of making vegetables the center of every meal (rather than meat), we guarantee your family will look, feel, and live better. "All the nutritional requirements that the human body has—all the vitamins, minerals, proteins, amino acids, enzymes, carbohydrates, and fatty acids that exist, that the human body needs to survive— are to be found in fruits and vegetables" (*Healthy Habits*).

The only downside to vegetables is that many are sprayed with pesticides to keep the bugs away, then treated with chemicals to insure they stay fresh on the trip to your local grocery store. It's better not to buy your vegetables from a national grocery store chain. Instead, look for local grocers, farmer's markets, and road- side stands that offer fresh, locally grown produce. If you can find farmers who grow their produce organically (without pesticides), so much the better.

The other thing to keep in mind about vegetables is that you can easily rob them of their nutrients by overcooking. To avoid that dan- ger, avoid baking, boiling, and, of course, frying. Instead, try steam- ing. You can purchase a very inexpensive collapsible metal steamer at a kitchen shop. Steaming is the best cooking method for retaining nutrients, and is really simple once you get the hang of it. Put an inch of water in the bottom of a pan and bring it to a boil. Drop in the steamer filled with vegetables. Tightly cover the pan and turn the heat down to medium. Most vegetables take between 10 to 20 minutes to steam, depending upon whether you like them crisp, crisp-tender, or very tender. Just remember, the crisper the healthier.

Bread, Cereal, Rice, and Pasta

It's so amusing to see the Food Pyramid printed on the back of white bread, instant rice, or children's cereal, as if these "foods" (and we use the term loosely) qualify as a nutritious part of your diet. In the so-called refining process, these "foods" have been so completely stripped of nutrients that they shouldn't even be called food. Refined foods are not only non-foods, they are anti-foods.

"Our foods are awash in naked calories, meaning that what used to be good food is now processed and refined to the point that the nutrients required for the assimilation of the food have been removed from it. Since the nutrients required for the food's absorption are gone, those nutrients will be taken from the body's own stores," according to Dr. Allan Spreen. The result is nutritional deficiencies. You can actually suffer from malnourishment even though you consume excess calories.

The key is eating WHOLE GRAIN products. Eat whole-grain bread, whole-grain pasta, and brown rice. To be honest, getting accustomed to the heavier texture of whole grain products takes a while. But once your taste buds adjust, you will wonder how you ever ate that wimpy, tasteless, nutritionless white stuff. Be patient.

Well, so much for the food pyramid! We hope we have opened your eyes to new ideas and the truth about good nutrition. Don't stop with the small amount of information provided in this short chapter. Visit your local bookstore and check out some of the resources listed below.

Eat Well, Live Well, Pamela Smith, Creation House*
Fit for Life by Harvey and Marilyn Diamond, Warner Books.
Food for Life, Pamela Smith, Creation House
Food Smart, Cheryl Townsley, Pinon Press
The Good Life, Pamela Smith, Creation House
Healthy Habits, David and Anne Frahm, Pinon Press
The 15-Minute Meal Planner, Emilie Barnes and Sue Gregg, Harvest House.

---

*Pamela Smith is a very popular nutritionist who advocates a more "mainstream" program than the one described in this chapter. That is, there's provision for poultry, dairy products, and the like. Your family may find her recipes much more palatable, especially when you are just making the switch to healthier eating. We prefer the vegetarian regimens presented by the Diamonds and Frahms, but it's pretty "drastic" and definitely takes some getting used to. Emilie Barnes is somewhere in between, and her book is delightful, informative, and easy to read.

The Food-Behavior Connection

Our neighbor Dr. Allan Spreen, "The Nutrition Physician," has been a family doctor for many years, and now devotes his time to sports nutrition and lecturing on the food-behavior connection. As a coach for a member of the American Olympic diving team (and advisor to numerous top athletes), he knows that an athlete's diet has a direct effect on his or her performance. What might surprise you is that Dr. Spreen insists that *everyone's* performance—in all aspects of life—is profoundly affected by diet. In his practice, he has observed that nutritional deficiencies often result in behavioral problems in children and irritability in adults.

If your family isn't active in a positive way, but is, in fact, *hyperactive*, it's time to look at nutritional culprits. "Right off the bat, you must remove non-food chemicals [especially caffeine] from your diet," says Dr. Spreen. "This is no joke, and the potential rewards of this simple step are well worth the effort. ALL artificial flavors, colors, preservatives (other than vitamin C), and enhancers (MSG, etc.) need to be removed for at least one week. One lifetime would be better."

Unfortunately, this is much easier said than done. There are literally thousands of chemicals and additives in our foods. In fact, the average American consumes three to six pounds of these a year (*Family Fitness Fun*). We can't avoid all of them, but at least we can eliminate as many as possible. We have discovered that Leah goes absolutely NUTS if she consumes anything with red food coloring, and the baby goes absolutely NUTS if Mommy eats anything with dairy products in it. It's a frustrating process, but you *can* uncover food culprits.

According to Dr. Spreen, if your family's mood and behavior gets *worse* in the first three to four days after you eliminate a particular food item, you are definitely on the right track. (Yes, you read that right. We know it sounds weird, but Dr. Spreen swears it's true!) "Assuming things are better after a week or so," he explains, "you can track down the offending agents by reintroducing them, one at a time, and observing the results. This act alone will make you a believer in the biochemical behavior solution."

Once you've dealt with the chemical offenders, the next thing to look for are offending foods. The culprits might even be foods you have always considered "excellent foods" and they are most likely foods you eat every day. Any food you or a family member craves must be eliminated for one full week. For some strange reason, the human body develops what feels like a "craving" for harmful foods. If you remove the suspected food and behavior *deteriorates* in the first few days, stick it out; you are onto something. Gradually, you will experience permanent behavior/mood improvement.

For More Information

Much of the information in this chapter was provided by Dr. Allan Spreen, who offers personal nutritional consultations via mail, fax, or the Internet. If you contact him, he'll obtain a complete medical history and have you complete some questionnaires. Based on a study of these, he will develop a personalized nutrition therapy to treat whatever's ailing you (or your kids). It includes dietary guidelines (what to eat and what to avoid); specific supplement recommendations (what to take, when and how); alternative therapies to consider (what they are and where to find them); plus a personal message on cassette tape. The cost is only $140 *if you say you're a friend of the Partows—which we hereby decree you to be.*

He also offers an eye-opening audiocassette tape, "Nutrition for Survival in a Civilized World" for $9.95 (postage and handling included). We *highly recommend it.* You can contact him at:

The Nutrition Physician
6636 E. Vanguard St.
Mesa, AZ 85215
E-mail: NutriMD@aol.com

> *Then God said, "I give you every seed-bearing plant on the face of the whole earth and every tree that has fruit with seed in it. They will be yours for food."*
> —Genesis 1:29

Discussion Questions

1. Discuss your reaction to the analysis of the food pyramid.

2. Which of the "food groups" should you eliminate, moderate, or increase?

Suggested Family Activities

1. Pin a copy of the food pyramid to a dart board and have some fun!

2. Create a new food pyramid which reflects the kind of foods you plan to eat.

3. Take a trip to the library or bookstore. Check out books on health and fitness.

4. Purchase a healthy cookbook.

5. Experiment with healthy recipes.

Active Family Journal

The world belongs to the energetic.
—Ralph Waldo Emerson

Record your reaction to the food pyramid exercise.

_____

_____

_____

_____

_____

_____

_____

_____

_____

_____

_____

_____

_____

_____

_____

_____

_____

_____

_____

_____

_____

_____

_____

_____

_____

_____

_____

Chapter 13

FUEL FOR YOUR ACTIVE FAMILY LIFESTYLE

Did you know you can help your body help itself? Well, you can. In this chapter you will discover specific, simple steps your family can immediately take to help your bodies function more efficiently. When thinking about what it takes to stay fit and healthy, most people turn to outside measures: lifting weights, running, aerobic classes. While those things are certainly helpful (if done properly), people often neglect the *inside* of their body. For maximum vitality, you especially need to take care of your bowels, bladder, lungs, and skin (*Fit for Life*). We will look at each in turn.

Bowels and Bladder

Your bowels and bladder are vital to your survival. They determine, in large measure, how much vitality you have. Do you know that it is possible to live your entire life without "washing out the inside" of your body? Americans place so much emphasis on cleansing the outside of our bodies, but we walk around with clogged insides. A body that isn't properly cleansed on a regular basis cannot perform at its best and is susceptible to all kinds of illnesses.

I hadn't cleansed my body in thirty-three years, and I had the poor health to prove it. I *constantly* had colds and flus, headaches, fatigue, strep throat, and a host of other ills. In fact, I was sick at least once a month. But when I began taking measures to cleanse my body internally, I noticed an immediate and dramatic difference. We'll describe the process in greater detail later in the chapter, but for now, we have to warn you that it can be painful. I first heard of this concept when I read *Fit for Life*, by Harvey and Marilyn Diamond (Warner Books). I knew immediately that I had a lot of cleansing to do, so I jumped into the plan with my usual zeal.

After a few days on the cleansing program, my body seemed to literally explode. I experienced severe vomiting and diarrhea, dizziness, and profuse sweating. I thought I was going to die. The book had warned that this might happen if you tried to make up for years of abuse and neglect too quickly. I should have taken the warning more seriously. But I followed their advice and resisted the temptation to treat the symptoms with prescription or over-the-counter drugs. Instead, I let my body do what it needed to do. And let me tell you, when it was over, I never felt better in my life. And for the next few months (until I went down for the count with morning sickness), I had more energy, vitality, and *joy* than I ever dreamed possible.

Does your family eat in ways that help your bodies cleanse themselves? Or do you eat in such a way that clogs your body? Now you may be wondering: what clogs the body? FAT! We know we've talked about the perils of fat already, but it just can't be emphasized strongly enough. God never designed your body to process the amount of fat that Americans consume. As a result, the fat clings to you. It clings to your thighs. It clings to your hips. It clings to your upper arms. Well, you know the spots. Meanwhile, the cholesterol literally clogs up your arteries. Not a pretty picture, is it? FAT CLOGS! And the absolute worst clogger of all is . . . red meat. If you want to get out of the business of clogging up your own body, the best thing you can do is completely eliminate red meat from your family's diet.

Now, what *cleanses* the body? The same thing we use to clean everything else. WATER! The human body is at least 70 percent water (*Fit for Life*). Therefore, it only makes sense to consume plenty of water. However, just drinking water isn't enough. "Drinking water won't [thoroughly] cleanse your body, because it does not carry the enzymes and other life-preserving elements into the body the way the water in fruits and vegetables can. Water transports the nutrients in food to all of the body's cells and in turn, removes toxic wastes." That's why fruits and vegetables are called "high water-content" foods and it's why you simply can't get enough of them.

Before you put anything into your mouth, ask yourself: is this food going to cleanse or clog my body? If the answer is clog, then don't eat it. You are not a prisoner of your taste buds, at least, you don't have to be. There is more to your life than that, isn't there? There's more to who you want to be and what you want to do with your life than pleasing those tyrants in your mouth. How can you ignore your whole mind, body, and soul for the sake of your taste buds? Here's what the apostle Paul said about people who live like that: "Their destiny is destruction, their god is their stomach, and their glory is in their shame. Their mind is on earthly things" (Philippians 3:19). Don't let your stomach or your taste buds be your god. Repeat after us:

> *I will not yield to the taste bud tyrants! I will not surrender! I will not be a taste bud prisoner!*

One other quick tip about helping your digestive system. There *is* a time to refrain from drinking and that is with meals. Do not drink anything—not even water—immediately before, during or after meals, because it dilutes the digestive juices in your stomach.

Lungs

Your lungs also play an important part in cleansing your body. Breathing is the one function of the human body that operates both automatically and voluntarily. That is, you breathe whether you think about it or not (automatic), much like your body digests food whether you think about it or not. Just like your heart pumps blood whether you think about it or not. However, you can also control your breathing voluntarily. Just as you can choose to lift your arm or move your head, you can consciously choose to breathe. Not only that, you can voluntarily control *how* you breathe.

It is a proven fact that you can enhance your body's ability to cleanse itself with the proper breathing technique. The key is taking long, deep breaths rather than the rapid, shallow breathing typical of most of us. The results of poor breathing technique include fatigue, diminished brain power, and weakened health. And you don't want those things for your active family, do you? To practice good breathing technique, your whole family can try the following exercise:

> Inhale for a count of 7
> Hold your breath for a count of 28
> Slowly release the air for a count of 14

Also keep in mind that the quality of the air you breathe is extremely important. If you live in the city, be sure to travel to the fresh air as often as you can. Remember, too, that the air in our homes and offices quickly becomes stagnant if we keep windows tightly shut. It is especially important to keep a window slightly cracked when you sleep at night and to periodically air out your entire house. Continually battle back the dust using your vacuum cleaner, not only on carpets but on light fixtures, furniture, curtains, windowsills, baseboards, air vents, and anywhere else dust particles might settle. (Replace carpets with tile, hardwood, or linoleum wherever possible; carpets are a breeding ground for dust and household toxins.) And speaking of air vents, be sure to change your air filters frequently. You might even consider investing in an electronic air cleaner.

Also, take a look at the types of household cleansers you use. Bleach, ammonia, and other chemicals used in most grocery-store-bought brands are extremely toxic. Instead, find a supplier of environmentally safe, biodegradable household cleaners. This small step will make a big difference in the quality of the air in your home.

Another simple thing you can do to improve the quality of the air your family breathes is to maintain a good number and variety of indoor houseplants. "According to research findings at the National Aeronautics and Space Administration, common houseplants can also help purify the air. Not only do plants such as English ivy, dracaenas, and palms freshen stale air, they also remove toxins such as benzene, formaldehyde, and carbon monoxide that can build up in any [home] from the use of paper products, cigarette smoke, cleaning and office supplies, natural gas, and so forth. . . . Although any plant will help, research has shown that Gerbera daisy, mother-in-law's tongue, pothos, and spider plants absorb the most toxins. NASA researcher B. C. Wolverton claims that eight to fifteen plants will 'significantly improve' the air quality in the average home. That's about one plant per 100 square feet."*

Skin

Americans don't like sweat. And when we are riding in an elevator or a crowded bus, we are really thankful for it. Nevertheless, sweat is yet another important way that the body cleanses itself of waste products and toxins. So the next time your family is playing together, bypass the antiperspirant and let your bodies release those toxins. You should plan to work up a sweat at least three times a week.

Another thing that has unfortunately become passé is bathing. Americans think a quick shower is the same as a bath, but it isn't. Be sure to let your children soak in a nice warm, chemical-free bath at least once a week. (Ditto for Mom and Dad.) Before and after bathing, you can slough off dead skin cells that clog pores and interfere with their work of cleansing. Use a pumice, loofah, or all-natural buffing product. Keep your skin clean and it will do the rest.

Paul and Sarah Edwards, *Working From Home* (Jeremy P. Tarcher, Inc.), p. 142.

Internal Cleansing Routine

As we have seen, the key to weight loss and vibrant health is your body's own elimination cycle. The body is God's masterpiece. If we simply aid the body (or at least, don't interfere with it) it will keep itself in wonderful working order. Here's a program your family can follow to "help you help your body help itself."

First thing in the morning, everyone in your family should drink eight to sixteen ounces of water. This signals the body to begin the work of cleansing. Then, if possible, go for a brisk walk or do some other moderate aerobic exercise together. Now everyone's ready for breakfast, so pour out big bowls of cereal with toast on the side . . . right? Well, not exactly. We'd like to suggest that you eat *nothing but fruit* until approximately noon.

The reason for eating only fruit in the morning is that it gives your body the opportunity to cleanse itself, to clear out everything you ate the day before and get a fresh start on the day. We were extremely skeptical of this plan, which is set forth in detail in *Fit for Life*, by Harvey and Marilyn Diamond. We had often heard it said, "Eat breakfast like a king, lunch like a prince, and dinner like a pauper." However, now that we have used this plan for a year or so, we are firm believers. We'd like to suggest a slight modification to the axiom: "Eat breakfast like *the King of Fruit*, lunch like a prince, and dinner like a pauper."

Some days we are hungry by 11:00 A.M., and that's fine. There's no need to be rigid; just use noon as a guideline. However, if you have a nice, large fruit shake for breakfast, don't be surprised if you are *not hungry again* until early afternoon. Enjoy a hearty lunch including plenty of vegetables and pasta or brown rice.

What if the children are in school all day? How can they follow the program? Pack them a nutritious lunch, rather than handing them money for pizza and soda, that's how. You can also pack an "emergency" supply of our "Good for You Cookies" (see chapter 16), just in case they can't hold out until the appointed lunch hour. They can quickly pop one in their mouth when the teacher's not looking. (We didn't write that . . . it just appeared on the page!)

Again, we know these changes are tough to make, but do the best you can. Even small changes in the right direction make a difference.

For dinner, you can round out the day with a light but nutritious meal of vegetables and whole grains. Then, no one should eat anything whatsoever after eight or nine P.M. (depending upon what time you retire for the evening). Be sure to allow at least two to three hours of time for digestion prior to sleep; otherwise the food in your stomach will putrefy, resulting in bad breath and bad health. Tell the kids, "No more snacks before bed!" (Then good luck enforcing it! Cameron is constantly sneaking light-night snacks to the kids, much to Donna's chargrin.)

Actually, you'll notice there's really no provision for snacks here. I used to sit at my computer snacking all day long. (I've got the crumbs lodged in my keyboard to prove it.) I thought snacking gave me more energy. It didn't! I kept eating and eating those snacks, trying to build energy. Funny thing, when I stopped snacking for energy I suddenly felt more energetic. Duh! Now, instead of pretzels, I reach for my water bottle. If you really must snack (and sometimes we must—especially if we are hiking or otherwise on-the-go and need an energy boost) reach for something nutritious.

If you are anything like us, you are extremely skeptical of this program. We wouldn't have believed any of this either. But we were desperate enough to give it a try. The turning point came when Donna's sister videotaped her from the rear. She was devastated, but Donna considers it a great favor. It gave her enough motivation to make changes for all of us. As a result, we have each lost approximately twenty pounds without dieting, and the whole family looks and feels better.

Will you do this: Set aside your skepticism and try it *for a week or two*? See how your family feels and judge for yourself. Do keep in mind this warning: if you have not cleansed or detoxified your body for many years, and you make these changes too quickly, your body may undergo a process called detoxification (Donna's description of her experience appears earlier in the chapter).

Detoxification can include severe diarrhea, profuse sweating, and even vomiting. Remember: *Do not treat these symptoms with over-the-counter drugs.* Your body is doing what you want it to do: it is ridding itself of toxins. (For more information on how to detox properly, read *Fit for Life*.)

What you *can* do, however, is take it slow. Make one change at a time. The best place to start is with your family's breakfast routine. Serve up the "Jump-start breakfast" (see chapter 16) every day for one week. Change lunch routines the following week. Around the third or fourth week, modify your dinner and gradually eliminate snacks. We promise you'll have a different family if you do!

Nevertheless, I will bring health and healing to it; I will heal my people and will let them enjoy abundant peace and security.
                                            —Jeremiah 33:6

Discussion Questions

1. Discuss what it means to "clean out" your body.

2. Discuss the role of the bowels, bladder, lungs, and skin in the cleansing process.

3. Discuss some ways that you clog rather than cleanse your body.

Suggested Family Activities

1. Practice the breathing technique.

2. Purify the air in your home: buy several plants, vacuum the house, purchase new air filters.

3. Plan for each family member to bathe at least once a week.

4. Make fruit shakes for breakfast every day this week.

5. Begin actively attempting to detoxify your body, using the procedures outlined here and in the book *Fit for Life*.

6. Develop a strategy for insuring that everyone drinks enough water each day. Here's a simple approach: buy each member a large sixteen-ounce drinking cup, then use a system to track how many times they refill the cup each day. (The goal, of course, would be to drink four full cups.) We have included a sample chart.

7. Plan to include high-water content foods in every meal.

8. Take a trip to a farmer's market or roadside fruit and vegetable stand. Begin experimenting with recipes featuring fresh food (rather than meat or dairy products).

Active Family Journal

He that masters breathing can walk on sand without leaving footprints.

—ancient Chinese proverb

Record your experience "clearing out your temples."

_____
_____
_____
_____
_____
_____
_____
_____
_____
_____
_____
_____
_____
_____
_____
_____
_____
_____
_____
_____
_____
_____
_____
_____
_____
_____
_____

Water Consumption Chart

Week of: _____
Goal: _____ glasses/cups per day

Sunday			
Monday			
Tuesday			
Wednesday			
Thursday			
Friday			
Saturday			

Note: Fill in the names of family members along top of column. Each time they refill their glass/cup, have them mark the chart in the appropriate box. Review at the end of the week.

Chapter 14

DIETING: THE BIG LIE

Have you ever noticed that the first three letters in the word diet are D-I-E? No wonder our body hears the word and says "No way!"

—paraphrase of Anthony Robbins

At the risk of sounding sexist, we're including this mini-chapter primarily for the benefit of you moms and teenage girls out there. With all this talk about how overweight people might have a tough time playing together (in the kind of healthy, active ways we're proposing), we're afraid you might think: "Gee, I'd better hurry up and go on a diet." Please DON'T.

At any given moment, an estimated 80 to 115 million Americans are on a diet of some kind. Would you believe that dieting is a $10 billion industry in the United States? Diets are the perfect example of the myth that it "has to hurt to work." Nothing could be further from the truth. Diets absolutely, positively DO NOT WORK. That's because when you take in less calories than your body needs to function, here's what happens:

1. You are tired, so you move less. (Not much energy for playing together, that's for sure.)
2. Your metabolism slows, so you burn less calories.
3. Your body uses lean muscle mass for fuel. Since muscle mass

burns calories, the less muscle mass you have, the less calories your body burns. That's why losing muscle mass is the most physically dangerous and counter-productive aspect of dieting. And make no mistake about it, if you diet, you *will* lose muscle mass and you *will* set yourself up for rapid weight gain in the very near future. Guaranteed.

4. Your body stores FAT to ward off starvation. That's right. Rather than "getting with the program" when you go on a diet, your fat cells run into hiding. Dieting *does not* reduce fat . . . it actually increases fat. Do you find yourself wondering why *anyone* would diet?

5. You crave high-calorie food, for both physical and psychological reasons. That's why almost all diets end with a binge. And when you return to normal eating, your fat cells throw a party and you end up weighing *more* than when you started the diet.

In short, when you diet you lose muscle and gain fat. That's exactly what *you don't want to do*. What you want to do is gain muscle and lose fat, and there isn't a crash diet in the world that can help you accomplish those goals. The problem is not *how much* we eat. The problem is *what* we eat. If you increase the amount of fruits and vegetables you eat, we personally guarantee: you WILL lose weight. If you keep it up, you will keep it off. And you'll do it in such a way that provides fuel for playing together, rather than draining you of needed energy.

"Eighty percent of calories [in the typical American diet] come from meat and dairy products, visible fats, sugar, syrup, and refined breads and cereals. A meager eight percent comes from fruits and vegetables. Yet from that lean amount comes 70 percent of our Vitamin C and 49.7 percent of our Vitamin A. If fruits and vegetables were increased to make up 50 percent of the total calories, the vitamin and mineral supply in our diet would increase six times" (*The Seventh-Day Diet*, by Chris Rucker and Jan Hoffman, Random House, 1991).

Say goodbye to the big lie! You do not have to starve yourself to look and feel great. A moderate exercise program, along with healthy eating habits will provide the fuel you require to become part of an active family.

I recently had the privilege of speaking at a large women's conference with Mrs. United States 1994-5, Sheri Rose Sheperd. When I heard she was my co-presenter, I secretly thought, "Oh, great, just what I need: Barbie with a Bible." Wow, was I wrong. What an incredible servant! What an incredibly beautiful woman! She shared with the audience that it wasn't always so. She once battled chronic fatigue syndrome, food addiction, bulimia, and depression. She's written a wonderful book, *Fit for Excellence*, that outlines how she lost sixty-five pounds "eating from the King's table." It's not a diet plan; it's a biblically based lifestyle plan. We think it's a great resource for families who want to *Play Together and Stay Fit Together*. To order a copy of the cookbook, call 800-877-LIFE or send $10.00 plus $3.00 shipping and handling to:

Remodeling America Ministries

15111 N. Hayden Road, #160-242

Scottsdale, AZ 85260

When you call, tell Sheri we sent you. And be sure to ask about Sheri's new weekend program, called Fit for Excellence.

For physical training is of some value, but godliness has value for all things, holding promise for both the present life and the life to come.
                                                                —1 Timothy 4:8

Discussion Questions

1. Does your experience with dieting reveal that you believe the lie "It has to hurt to work"? Let each member discuss their past attitudes.

2. If members of your family have tried dieting, let them discuss their experiences.

Suggested Family Activities

1. Don't diet!

2. Throw out any diet books you've accumulated over the years!

Active Family Journal

For the eyes of the Lord range throughout the earth to strengthen those whose hearts are fully committed to him.
—2 Chronicles 16:9

Record your reaction to changing eating habits instead of "dieting."

_____
_____
_____
_____
_____
_____
_____
_____
_____
_____
_____
_____
_____
_____
_____
_____
_____
_____
_____
_____
_____
_____
_____
_____
_____

Chapter 15

RECIPES FOR AN ACTIVE FAMILY

Eat to live, not live to eat.

—Benjamin Franklin

Just for fun, we thought we'd share some of our family's favorite healthy recipes with you. At the end of the chapter, we've listed some good healthy cookbooks you might want to investigate—since you can't live on fruit shakes and "Good for You Cookies" forever. (Actually, *Donna* can live on 'em indefinitely, but we're talking to you *normal* people now!) Meanwhile, here're some ideas to get you cookin' right:

Breakfasts

Jump-Start Breakfast

½ cup orange juice
1 banana
1-2 pints strawberries (you can substitute frozen strawberries)
4 ice cubes

Toss everything in the blender until smooth.

Strawberry Shake With Almond Milk

Put the following in the blender for 3 minutes:
¼ cup almonds

1 cup cold water
2 tsp. maple syrup
Add and blend until thick and creamy:
2 frozen bananas (Note: best to peel before freezing)
6 fresh or frozen strawberries (add more if desired)

Lunches

Nikki's Legendary Peanut Butter Roll-ups

Fat-free flour tortillas
All-Natural crunch peanut butter
Breadshop brand oat bran granola
Honey
Cinnamon

Spread peanut butter on a flat tortilla. Add a layer of granola.
Drizzle with honey and sprinkle with cinnamon. Rool up, slice
and enjoy!

Stuffed Pita

1 package of oat bran pita bread
10 slices of turkey
1 package fat-free cream cheese
2 T. chives
2 T. basil

Cut pita bread in half. Combine softened cream cheese in a
small bowl with chives and basil. Spread a thin layer inside each
pita, then add a slice of turkey.

Oat Pita With Hummus

2 cups cooked garbanzo beans
⅓ cup water
¼ cup tahini (sesame seed butter)
¼ cup lemon juice

4 cloves garlic, crushed
1 T. olive oil
2 tsp. onion powder
1 tsp. salt

Place all ingredients in blender; blend until smooth. Serve on warm pita bread.

Fresh Fries and Salad

Slice potatoes thin. Spray with Pam and sprinkle with Vege-Sal, garlic salt, onion powder, and paprika. Broil until brown, approximately five minutes. (Flip and brown the other side, if desired.) Serve with salad.

Dinners

Awesome (Meatless) Burgers

4 cups water
½ cup soy sauce
⅓ cup canola oil
1 cup chopped pecans
¼ cup nutritional yeast flakes
2 tsp. garlic powder
2 tsp. onion powder
1 tsp. bacon bits
1 tsp. ground coriander
4 cups rolled oats

Place all ingredients (EXCEPT rolled oats) in large pan, stir well and bring to a slow boil over medium heat. Stir in rolled oats and remove from heat. Cover and let cool. Form into burger patties. Bake on oiled baking sheets for 15 minutes on each side in oven preheated to 350°. Serve on whole wheat buns. These freeze and reheat exceptionally well.

Pesto Sauce

½ cup pine nuts
¼ cup olive oil
⅓ cup water
¼ cup lemon juice
¼–½ cup fresh or dried sweet basil leaves
1 tsp. garlic salt

Mix together and serve over your choice of pasta.

Zucchini and Carrot With Pesto

6 large carrots, peeled and cut in thin strips
3 large zucchini, peeled and cut in thin strips

Cook in steamer or in ½ inch of boiling water in saucepan.
NOTE: Carrots require 3–4 minutes *more* than the zucchini,
so put them in steamer/pan first. Serve with Pesto Sauce.

Cauli-Broccoli With Cashew Gravy

1 cup brown rice
2 cups cauliflower florets
2 cups broccoli florets

Cook brown rice according to package directions. Lightly
steam or microwave the cauliflower and broccoli in small
amount of water. Meanwhile prepare gravy as follows:

2 cups warm water
½ cup raw cashews
2 T. nutritional yeast flakes
2 T. soy sauce
1 T. canola oil
1 package Lipton onion-mushroom soup
2 tsp. onion powder
2 tsp. bacon bits

½ tsp. Vege-Sal

½ tsp. garlic powder

½ cup onion

Place all ingredients in blender; blend four minutes. Pour in pan and simmer over low heat for 10 minutes. Serve over rice and vegetables.

Nutritious Snacks

Popsicles

2 cups yogurt

1 can frozen orange juice concentrate

2 tsp. vanilla

Mix. Pour into plastic popsicle molds and freeze.

"Ice Cream"

Equal amounts of milk (nut or rice milk preferred) and orange juice. Sweeten with honey or a small amount of fructose, if desired. Freeze and enjoy!

The Famous "Good-for-You" Cookies

2 cups whole-grain cereal flakes

1 cup whole wheat pastry flour

1 cup rolled oats

1 cup raisins

¾ cup chopped pecans

½ cup raw sunflower seeds

½ cup shredded coconut

½ cup canola oil

½ cup honey

¼ cup liquid egg substitute

1 tsp. ground coriander

2 tsp. vanilla extract

½ tsp. salt

Preheat oven to 350°. In large bowl mix together cereal, flour, oats, raisins, pecans, sunflower seeds, and coconut. Blend remaining ingredients together in small bowl. Pour liquid over dry mixture and mix well. Refrigerate until chilled. Bake on lightly greased cookie sheet for 10 to 15 minutes (the longer they bake, the crunchier they get; watch closely for burning).

Banana Nut Cookies

4 very ripe bananas
2 cups rolled oats
1 cup chopped pecans
½ cup chopped almonds
1 cup chopped, pitted dates
⅓ cup frozen orange juice concentrate, thawed
⅓ cup canola oil
½ tsp. almond extract
½ tsp. salt
½ tsp. cinnamon

Preheat oven to 325°. Mix all ingredients thoroughly in a large bowl and let stand for about six minutes. Drop cookies by large spoonfuls onto lightly oiled baking sheet. Bake 30 minutes or until golden brown.

Crunch Coffee Cake

1 cup Breadship brand oat bran granola
2 cups whole wheat flour
1 T. baking powder
2 tsp. cinnamon
⅓ cup honey
2 beated egg whites (or substitute)
½ cup soy or rice milk

½ cup canola oil
2 tsp. shredded orange peel
½ cup apple juice

Preheat oven to 375°. Stir together granola, flour, baking powder, and cinnamon. In a separate bowl, combine egg, milk, oil, and honey. Add to the dry ingredients and mix well. Combine orange peel and apple juice and stir into combined ingredients. Spread evenly in a greased pan. Bake 30 minutes.

Cinnamon Tasties

3 medium fat-free flour tortillas
3 tsp. cinnamon

Preheat oven to 375°. Cut tortillas into thin, narrow strips and sprinkle with cinnamon. Bake until crisp (about 3 to 4 minutes).

Recommended Cookbooks

Eating Better Cookbooks, self-published by Sue Gregg and Emilie Barnes. The series includes six cookbooks: Main Dishes, Casserole Meals in Minutes, Soups and Muffins, Breakfasts, Lunches and Snacks, and Desserts. Write to:

Sue Gregg's Eating Better Cookbooks
8830 Glencoe Drive
Riverside, CA 92503
1-909-687-5491

The Seventh-Day Diet: How the Healthiest People in America Live Better, Longer, Slimmer & Why, by Chris Rucker and Jan Hoffman (Random House). We have *loved* every recipe we have tried from this book, which is actually much more than a cookbook. Very highly recommended.

Fit for Life and *Living Health*, by Harvey and Marilyn Diamond

(Warner Books), also include many excellent recipes. These books are *must reading* if you are serious about making the kind of life-style changes we've introduced here.

Eat Well, Live Well and *Food for Life*, by Pamela Smith (Creation House). These are absolutely beautiful books (great to put on a coffee table even if you never use them!), with recipes your family will love.

Chapter 16

A FINAL WORD

God cannot be mocked. A man reaps what he sows.

—Galatians 6:7

In closing, we'd like to tell you a tale of two people coming into the home stretch of life. The first lived life the American way: eating whatever tasted good, doing whatever seemed convenient for the moment. We'll call him Bob. The other lived out the principles shared in this book: eating right, exercising, approaching each new day with a sense of adventure. His name is Warren Faidley.

At the age of sixty-seven, Bob struggles just to walk from room to room. Actually, getting out of his chair is his most significant daily challenge. His energy level is non-existent. His typical day starts off with a few cups of coffee (with plenty of cream and sugar) and a donut or two. Around noontime, he'll have a lunchmeat sandwich smothered with butter and mayonnaise and chase it down with some soda or iced tea. Dinner is meat and potatoes, of course. He snacks on cookies and cakes all day long in front of the television set. His exercise routine consists of clicking the remote control.

Bob has battled diabetes, cancer, and coronary artery disease. He has had blood clots and tumors. He has suffered two heart at-tacks, had quadruple bypass surgery, and those are just the ones we can remember. Truth be told, he has been in-and-out of the hospital his entire adult life, turning over most of his money to doctors, hos-pitals, and pharmacies. Footing the bills for his unending health problems has literally driven him to bankruptcy. The saddest part of this tale *is that it's so typical*! The senior citizen who *doesn't* identify with much (or all) of Bob's story is the exception.

Most of Bob's (now-grown) children are overweight and in poor health. Now, his grandchildren are repeating the lifestyle pattern of watching television and munching potato chips. They call it "the good life." It doesn't seem that good to us.

We recently suggested to Bob that perhaps some "dietary modifications" might be in order. He chuckled and dipped another fudge-covered-Oreo into a glass of whole milk. Then brushing off our comments with a wave of his hand, he said, "Hey, I'm going to *enjoy* my life." Enjoy? Are we missing something here? If that's *enjoying life*, let's all check out right now. It ain't worth the price of living. Fortunately, we don't believe Bob. We don't believe there's nothing more to this life than indulging our taste buds and resting in our easy chairs.

Warren Earl Faidley is living proof that there's more—much more.

We met Warren when we vacationed at Tanque Verde Ranch in Tucson, Arizon.* The first thing that impressed us about Warren was his bright cheery smile and positive attitude toward life; then we couldn't help noticing that he was in perfect physical condition. (He could put most teenagers—and many professional athletes—to shame.) Over breakfast one morning, as Warren ate a plateful of fresh fruit, he told us of his big plans to become a sailor. At the age of sixty-three, after retiring from thirty-four years with the Air Force, he is now getting certified as a crew member on sailing cruises. His first trip will be a four-day tour of the North Channel Islands off the California coast, but he has even bigger plans. "My dream is to have my own yacht someday and maybe live on the Sea of Cortez down in Mexico. What I'd really like to do is sail across the Pacific to Australia."

Warren says he was not always the picture of vim and vigor. "My

---

*Tanque Verde is a dude ranch and four-star hotel all rolled into one. We highly recommend it for your next "active family vacation." Call 800-234-DUDE and tell Warren we sent you.

wife was a southern belle and cooked wonderful feasts, which of course I ate. Then I sat at a desk in front of a computer all day. It wasn't a healthy combination. When my wife died in 1991, of Lou Gehrig's disease, I decided to change my life. I had high blood pressure and cholesterol problems, but I was determined that I wasn't going to shorten my life if I could help it. It took six months of constant hiking here in the mountains near my home [in Tucson, Arizona], before my doctor said I was in the condition I was at seventeen years old. I was hiking thirty-five miles a week on rigorous terrain and even doing some jogging on the trails."

Warren also began modifying his rich diet. "I started reading labels, especially looking for fat content. That's the killer in modern man's diet. We have to realize, we're not busy like we used to be on farms. We live a sedentary life and we need to adjust our diet accordingly."

Warren is convinced that life can and should be a great adventure . . . if you're in good enough condition to enjoy it. He certainly is. His "retirement" lifestyle is anything but "retiring." Four days a week, he is up by six o'clock, has a light breakfast, then heads to the ranch to meet the guests. Afterwards, he leads a six-mile hike into the Rincorn Mountains. He returns at noon for a very light lunch, consisting mostly of fruits and vegetables. From 1:00 to 3:00 P.M., he sketches with guests, and heads home by 3:30. On weekends, he usually travels to San Diego to sail.

We asked Warren if he could offer some final advice to young moms and dads like us. Here's what he said: "As you're bringing up your children, you've got to be a role model. For them to respect you, you have to treat yourself properly. Take time to exercise each day and bring them along with you. More important than Little League and Scouts, is the time you could spend one-on-one, maybe walking and talking in the evening. It doesn't have to cost a penny. If you're a couch potato and you let yourself go, and you don't have an interesting life, then you cripple your children. They won't take your advice; they won't be the person they could be. Even if you don't care about yourself, if you care about your children, make the lifestyle changes."

We couldn't have said it better ourselves.

We hope you get to visit Tanque Verde Ranch and meet Warren someday. We know he'll be an inspiration to you. In the meantime, love your life and love your children enough to begin building the same kind of active lifestyle for your family.

Put this book down, get up out of your easy chair, and *begin.*

Be very careful, then, how you live—not as unwise but as wise, making the most of every opportunity, because the days are evil.

—Ephesians 5:15-16

MORE IDEAS TO HELP YOUR FAMILY PLAY TOGETHER

Chapter 17

CHEAP TRAVEL RESOURCES

All the exciting national and international adventure opportunitites we described in chapters 5 and 6 may have been overwhelming. Let's be truthful—they *are* expensive. And although we have had the privilege of active family trips, you won't find the Partows claiming many frequent flyer prizes for miles racked up on foreign adventures.

What if you simply can't *afford* a week-long rafting or a dude ranch experience? What about families who'll *never* take an African safari or trek the Himalayas?

First of all, you may have more money available than you think. We plan and save. And we use what money we do have to become an active family. It's our priority because it's the best gift we can give our children. Frankly, money that we refuse to waste on junk food, family-room-shaking entertainment systems, useless exercise gadgets, and what we earlier called "hyper-activities" goes a long way toward funding more healthy activities. It's a *redirection of existing resources.*

Secondly, those big trips may be once-in-lifetime opportunities for your family to play together. They may be something that even has to wait until later for you and your spouse—say, a twenty-fifth anniversary celebration or when the kids leave the nest. Here's the point: *Do the smaller, less expensive things now.* You want to be around to enjoy the "big" things later, don't you?

Most importantly, you have active, affordable travel opportunities right in your backyard. The secret to affordable active fun is America's state and national parks. We are amazed by the wealth of opportunities for family fun and adventure these parks offer. Everything from the obvious, like hiking and biking, to the more obscure, like kayaking and lean-to camping.

Just to get you started, we've compiled a state-by-state listing featuring at least one national and one state park for each, along with the 800-number to call for tourist information. Use this as a starting point to investigate your next family adventure—whether you're planning some weekend fun or next year's vacation— whether you're looking for something to do in your own state or places you plan to visit. Have fun playing together!

Nationwide

National Park Service
P.O. Box 37127
Washington, D.C. 20013–7127

Mistix
800–365–2267
Reservations for campsites at a dozen national parks throughout the country.

Alabama

Alabama Tourism and Travel, 800-ALA-BAMA

Alabama State Parks, 800-ALA-PARK

DeSoto State Park, Fort Payne, 205–845–0051
5,067 acres along Little River Canyon, one of the deepest gorges east of the Mississippi. Rock A resort area offers a lodge, chalets, and cabins. Modern and wilderness campsites are also available.

Dense woodlands and seasonal wildflowers appeal to hikers, while scenic highlights include Lookout Mountain and the 108-foot De-Soto Falls. Rock climbing is popular.

Talladega National Forest, Talladega, 205-362-2909
376,000 acres of hiking trails, camping, hunting, fishing, shooting ranges, a wilderness area, firewood cutting areas, and designated roads for off-road vehicles. Hiking, camping, and fishing are allowed in the 7,400-acre Cheaha Wilderness, but motorized vehicles and bicycles are prohibited. The Talladega Scenic Byway winds twenty-three miles along the backbone of the southern Appalachian Mountains, reaching an elevation of 2,407 feet.

Alaska
Fairbanks Visitors Information, 800-327-5774

Admiralty Island National Monument and Tongass National Forest, Juneau, 907-586-8751
Coastal rain forests, wild berry thickets, alpine meadows, freshwater lakes and streams; also harbor beavers, river otters, martens, weasels, mink, geese, and trumpeter and whistling swans. One of the greatest known concentrations of bald eagles in North America nests in trees and snags along the island's coast. Hiking, photography, fishing, wildlife viewing, wilderness camping, and crabbing are favored activities.

Denali State Park
At 324,240 acres, nearly half the size of Rhode Island, the park's terrain ranges from mile-high mountains and valley glaciers to the broad Chulitna River Valley. There are more than 100 miles of hiking trails for every level of ability; both backpackers and day hikers find breathtaking views of Mount McKinley, also known by its Native American name, Denali. Kayaking, cross-country skiing, and fishing available.

Arizona

Arizona Tourism, 800-842-8257

Grand Canyon National Park, Grand Canyon, 602-638-7771
   Camping available along the rim and down in the canyon. For
lodging call 602-638-2401 (South Rim) or 801-586-7686 (North
Rim). One mile deep, eight miles wide, and stretching 260 miles,
the canyon is one of the "seven wonders of the world." Hiking,
backpacking, mule trips, rafting, and motor-boating offered.

Red Rock State Park in Sedona, 602-282-6907
   286-acre park featuring spectacular views of the giant "red
rocks." No overnight accommodations in the park; however, camping is available nearby.

Prescott National Forest, Prescott, 520-445-1762
   1,237,000 acres with twelve campgrounds, including one for
horseback riders, and five picnic areas. For the hiker, backpacker,
horseback rider, or mountain biker, the forest offers nearly 450
miles of trails.

Arkansas

Arkansas Dept. of Parks & Tourism, 800-NATURAL

White River National Wildlife Refuge, DeWitt, 501-946-1468
   155,126 acres of bottomland, hardwood forests, and wetlands.
The many native animals at the refuge include black bears, deer,
squirrels, turkeys, and waterfowl. Twenty-five to thirty primitive
campsites are available. Fishing, boating, and hunting during certain seasons.

Lake Catherine State Park in Hot Springs
   2,180-acre lake park offers camping, canoeing, paddleboats, and
pontoons.

Scott Valley Resort & Guest Ranch in Mountain Home, 501-425-
5136
   Affordable dude ranch experiences, even for city slickers.

California

California Tourism, 800-GO-CALIF

Yosemite National Park, Yosemite, 209-372-0200
Famous for waterfalls, cliffs, giant sequoias, and unusual rock formations. Reservations are required at about half of the park's fifteen campgrounds and may be made up to eight weeks in advance. A camping stay is limited to seven days during summer. Permits are required for overnight backpacking trips in the wilderness. Quotas are set for the number of people who may begin an overnight trip from each trailhead. Up to 50 percent of the slots may be reserved up to six months in advance. Mail requests, along with $3.00, to Wilderness Reservations, Wilderness Center, P.O. Box 545, Yosemite, Calif. 95389, or call 209-372-0740. Cyclists are restricted to paved bikeways and park roads. Eight miles of bikeway wind through the eastern end of the valley.

Del Norte Coast Redwoods State Park, Crescent City, 707-445-6547
Unique combination of ancient redwoods and spectacularly scenic coastline. Activities at this 6,400-acre park include hiking, fishing, and horseback riding. The 145-site campground nestles in a grove of redwoods with a thick ground cover of ferns and unique native plants.

Channel Islands National Park, Ventura, 805-658-5730
This chain of eight islands is the habitat of blue whales, sea lions, and peregrine falcons. Island topography varies from volcanic rock to wind-swept cliffs, sandy beaches to dense kelp forests. All the islands have hiking trails. Camping permits required.

Summit Adventure in Bass Lake, 800-827-1282
Christian adventure camp for families; children must be over six.

Colorado

Colorado Tourism Information, 800-265-6723

Rocky Mountain National Park, Estes Park, 970-586-1206 or 800-365-2267

265,197 acres offering some of the most spectacular landscapes in the nation. Visitors can hike, mountaineer, camp, bike, cross-country ski, or ride horseback through this vast wilderness. The 50-mile Trail Ridge Road crosses the park from east to west, reaching 12,183 feet above sea level in near-arctic conditions. Several campgrounds; three are open year-round.

Golden Gate Canyon State Park, Golden, 303-582-3707
Ranges in elevation from 7,600 to 10,400 feet and covers 14,000 acres. Thirty-five miles of trails are shared by hikers, mountain bikers, and equestrians. There are more than 150 developed campsites, as well as backcountry shelters and tent sites. Ponds are stocked with trout, and there are streams suited for fly fishing. Wildlife includes bears, bobcats, and mountain lions.

Colorado Dude and Guest Ranch Association
P.O. Box 300
Tabernash, CO 80478
303-724-3653
Free directory of ranches.

Connecticut

Connecticut Tourist Information, 800-CT-BOUND

Hammonasset State Park in Madison, 203-245-2785
The state's largest public beach (two miles long) offers swimming, fishing, walking, and biking.

Macedonia Brook State Park, Kent, 860-927-3238
2,300 acres comprising a deep valley with Macedonia Brook at its center, surrounded by mountains. The brook is stocked with trout. Eighty-four campsites available from April to September and fifteen miles of easy to moderate trails. Natural inhabitants are bears, bobcats, turkeys, and red-tailed hawks.

Delaware

Delaware Tourism Office, 800-441-8846

Bombay Hook National Wildlife Refuge, Smyrna, 302-653-9345

15,122 acres, nearly three-quarters of which is tidal marsh. The refuge is a primary habitat for migrating and wintering ducks and northbound migrating geese.

Brandywine Creek State Park, Wilmington, 302-577-3534
Twelve miles of trails for walking, biking, and wildlife observation. Canoeing, tubing, and fishing are popular activities on Brandywine Creek. Bird walks, nature tours, and other public programs are held on weekends.

Killens Pond State Park, Felton, 302-284-4526
878-acre scenic park offers boating opportunities and fishing for largemouth bass, catfish, carp, perch, crappie, bluegills, and pickerel. Canoe, rowboat, and pedal boat during the summer. Other facilities include swimming pools, hiking trails, ball fields, and an eighteen-hole golf course. Picnic areas and a campground are also available.

Florida
Florida Keys Visitors Information, 800-FLA-KEYS

Everglades National Park, Homestead, 305-242-7700 or 800-388-9669
1.4 million acres can be explored on boardwalks, hiking trails and canoe and kayak trails. Long Pine Key, Flamingo, and Chekika campgrounds offer various services. The only lodging within the park is at Flamingo Point. Wildlife includes the elusive and extremely endangered Florida panther, snakes, alligators, crocodiles, and a wide array of birdlife. A permit is required for wilderness backpacking.

Homosassa Springs State Wildlife Park, Homosassa, 904-628-2311
This 150-acre wildlife park offers a rare opportunity to observe native Florida wildlife in a natural setting. There are manatees, alligators, crocodiles, snakes, bobcats, cougars, birds, and a huge spring, bubbling millions of gallons of water every hour. Nature

trails, boat tours, and a floating observatory to view fish and the endangered manatee.

Gamble Rogers State Park at Flagler Beach, 904-439-2474
Camp on the beach, where you can view the sea turtles, dolphins, and manatees.

Bahia Honda State Park on Big Pine Key, 305-872-2353
Hiking, snorkeling, kayaking, bicycling, and boating. Tent sites are $24.00; cabins $124.00 per night.

Georgia
Georgia Tourism, 800-VISIT-GA

Chattahoochee National Forest, Gainesville, 404-536-0541
750,000 mountainous acres feature waterfalls, sparkling mountain streams, hiking trails, lakes, and rivers. Beautiful scenery and many recreational opportunities. Kayakers and rafters shoot the rapids of the Chattooga Wild and Scenic River, one of the longest and least developed free-flowing rivers in the southeast. Or hike the challenging Appalachian Trail.

Cloudland Canyon State Park, Rising Fawn, 706-657-4050
Located on the western edge of Lookout Mountain. Hike the 4.5-mile West Rim and Waterfalls Trail, backpack on a 6.5-mile backcountry trail, picnic, camp, and swim. There are tent and trailer sites, walk-in campsites, cottages, and swimming pools.

Panola Mountain State Park in Stockbridge, 404-389-7801
600-acre park offers ranger walks and special wildlife programs. No overnight camping.

Hawaii
Maui Visitors Bureau, 800-525-MAUI

Haleakala National Park, Makawao, Maui, 808-572-9306
Rangers lead crater-rim walks at this ancient volcano, and visitors can ride horseback or hike on short self-guided trails or longer

ones that traverse the giant crater. Camping in the crater is by permit only and restricted to cabins and established campsites. Cabins must be reserved in advance. In the lush, green Kipahulu coast area, visitors can hike to scenic waterfalls and swim in pools along the Ohe'o Gulch. There are primitive campsites along the ocean.

Waimea Canyon and Koke'e State Park, Waimea, 808-335-5871
The "Grand Canyon of Hawaii" stretches ten miles from Captain Cook's landing site to Koke'e State Park. Hiking trails in the park offer unparalleled views of the canyon and Kauai's rare upland forest environment. The canyon itself is also accessible for hiking, fishing, and camping. Koke'e State Park and Waimea Canyon are administered by the state's parks and wildlife agencies, respectively.

Idaho
Idaho Travel Council, 800-VISIT-ID

Yellowstone National Park
Info: 307-344-7381
Reservations: 307-344-7311
The world's oldest national park, Yellowstone contains 2.2 million acres and features the famous canyon, geysers, and hot springs. The park's major scenic attractions line the 142-mile Grand Loop Road. Many of the most famous geysers and hot springs are on the west side of the park along the fifty-mile stretch between Mammoth Hot Springs and Old Faithful. Warming huts and visitor centers serve cross-country skiers and snowmobilers in winter. There are twelve campgrounds.

Bear Lake State Park and National Wildlife Refuge, Montpelier, 208-847-1757
Twenty miles long and eight miles wide, the park straddles the Idaho-Utah border in the southeast corner of Idaho. Surrounding the lake are a state park, the Cache National Forest, the Caribou National Forest, and the 17,600-acre Bear Lake National Wildlife Refuge. Camping, swimming, and boating are available.

Caribou National Forest, Pocatello, 208-236-7500

Covers more than one million acres and offers camping, hiking, backpacking, fishing, snowmobiling, horseback riding, and mountain biking. There are twenty-eight developed campgrounds, 1,200 miles of hiking and backpacking trails, several cross-country skiing and snowmobile trails, and a downhill ski area.

Illinois

Illinois Tourist Information, 800-223-0121

Shawnee National Forest, Harrisburg, 618-253-7114

273,800 acres of forested hills, lakes, and outcroppings of sandstone and limestone in the southern tip of Illinois. On the western edge of the forest, the LaRue Pine Hills area is rich ecologically, with 1,150 plant species, twenty-four amphibious animals, thirty-five reptiles, 173 birds, and about forty mammals. Visitors hike and ride horseback on 338 miles of trails. Fishing, rock climbing, camping, and picnicking are also popular.

Illinois Beach State Park, Zion, 708-662-4811

4,160-acre park includes dunes, marshes, and woodlands, and harbors a wide variety of wildlife, much of it threatened or endangered. More than 650 plant species, including prickly pear cactus, have been documented in the dunes area alone. There are about twenty miles of park trails, with ten open to cyclists. Snowshoeing and cross-country skiing are also practiced in the park. Swimming is a major attraction. Canoes may be carried into the lake. Fishing is permitted both in the lake and in small inland ponds. There are 244 developed campsites and a lodge scheduled to open in 1996.

Indiana

Indiana Tourist Information, 800-289-6646

Brown County State Park, Nashville, 812-988-6406

15,000 acres of rolling hills and beautiful forests, with twelve miles of dedicated hiking trails and another 80 miles of trails shared with equestrians. Recreational activities include cross-country skiing, snowshoeing, picnicking, guided nature programs, canoeing, and motor boating.

Hoosier National Forest, Bedford, 812-275-5987
189,000 acres of camping, hiking, backpacking, rock climbing, and fishing. The forest's popular 1,200-acre Hardin Ridge Recreation Area, situated on the shores of Monroe Reservoir, offers camping, picnicking, boat launches, swimming, nature walks, and interpretive programs and displays. Sundance Lake, a beautiful, 5.3-acre lake constructed in 1992, is stocked with bluegill, bass, and channel catfish, and offers some of the best fishing opportunities in the area.

Iowa
Iowa Tourism, 800-345-IOWA

Upper Mississippi River National Wildlife & Fish Refuge, McGregor, 319-873-3423
One hundred miles of scenic riverway for wildlife observation, camping, fishing, and boating. During the spring and fall migration seasons, visitors are most likely to see waterfowl in large numbers. Eagles are common in winter months. Great blue herons, great egrets, and other waterbirds make their nests on the refuge.

Brushy Creek State Recreation Area, Lehigh, 515-359-2501
Sixty miles of trails shared by hikers, equestrians, cross-country skiers, and snowshoers. The park is especially popular with horseback riders, and an equestrian campground has hitch rails and water. Another campsite is available to tenters along Brushy Creek. Smallmouth bass and panfish are plentiful in the creek. The park also includes a reserve for game hunters.

Kansas
Kansas Travel Information, 800-252-6727

Flint Hills National Wildlife Refuge, Hartford, 316-392-5553
Uplands, grasslands, agricultural lands, hardwood river bot-

toms, marshes, and flooded sloughs. The bird-watching on the refuge is best in April and May, and in November for the migration of waterfowl. The 18,000-acre refuge is also home to bald eagles.

Kanopolis State Park in Marquette, 913-546-2565
1,600 acres with hiking and biking trails and 120 campsites.

Kentucky
Kentucky Travel Information, 800-225-TRIP

Cumberland Gap National Historic Park, Middlesboro, 606-248-2817
Daniel Boone passed through the gap for the first time in 1769. 20,000-acre park featuring five campgrounds, four of which require backpacking permits and are accessible by foot only. Fifty miles of hiking trails ranging from short, self-guided nature trails to longer overnight trails. Horses and bikes permitted on many trails. The historic Hensley Settlement, accessible by trail or unpaved road, recreates life on an isolated farm during the early 1900s.

John James Audubon State Park, Henderson, 502-826-2247
Cottages available for rent on 697 acres of rolling hills. Features hiking, golfing, and tennis.

Louisiana
Louisiana Tourism, 800-33-GUMBO

Kisatchie National Forest, Pineville, 318-473-7160
600,000 acres including white sand beaches, rocky rapids, sandy bottomland covered with large hardwood and pine forests and mysterious, moss-draped swamps. Both developed and primitive campgrounds. Among Kisatchie's trails are the thirty-one-mile Wild Azalea National Recreation Trail, with a profusion of delicate pink azalea blossoms; or the Lakeshore Trail, shaded by a canopy of large oak, hickory, and beech trees.

Bayou Segnette State Park, Westwego, 504-736-7140
Campsites and cabins are available on 580 acres. Hiking and canoeing amidst alligators, snakes, and other bayou creatures.

Maine

Maine Tourism Information, 800-533-9595

Acadia National Park, Bar Harbor, 207-288-3338 or 800-365-2267
35,000 acres featuring soaring granite cliffs, beaches, and miles of scenic bike paths. Seven mountain peaks offer excellent ocean views and hiking paths.

Cobscook Bay State Park in Edmunds Township, 207-726-4412
Camping amidst nearly 900 acres along the coast, with views of bald eagles, seals, and moose, plus free clamming.

Maryland

Maryland Tourist Information, 800-543-1036

Assateague Island National Seashore, 800-365-2267

Assateague Island National Seashore, Berlin, 410-641-1441
The famous Chincoteague Wild Pony Roundup and related festivities occur each July. The area is a winter home for many migratory birds. Several year-round primitive campgrounds along the shore.

Patapsco Valley State Park, Ellicott City, 410-461-5005
15,000-acre park whose primary "trail" is the Patapsco River, traveled by canoe, tube, and kayak. The park is made up of five separate areas along thirty-two miles of the river. The park is largely wooded, with some steep stretches along the thirty miles of trails shared by hikers, cyclists, and equestrians. There are more than seventy seasonal campsites.

Massachusetts

Massachusetts Travel and Tourism Office, 800-227-6277

Great Meadows National Wildlife Refuge, Sudbury, 508-443-4661

Twelve miles of the Concord and Sudbury rivers, once a haunt of Henry David Thoreau. Now a sanctuary for more than 221 species of birds, as well as muskrats, foxes, raccoons, cottontail rabbits, weasels, squirrels, and various other small mammals.

Nickerson State Park, Brewster, 508-896-3491
1,955-acre park along the coast of Cape Cod has access to both salt and fresh water for power boaters, canoeists, and kayakers. Eight miles of bike paths and six miles of easy to intermediate hiking trails. In winter, there's cross-country skiing. 420 campsites with reservation lead time of about six months.

Michigan
Michigan Travel Bureau, 800-5432-YES

Isle Royale National Park, Houghton, 906-482-0984
571,790 acres of island wilderness in northern Lake Superior, accessible only by floatplanes and boats. Renowned for supporting one of the Midwest's few surviving wolf packs. It is also home to moose, red foxes, beavers, and hares. Hiking, camping, fishing, boating, scuba diving, and swimming.

Ludington State Park, Ludington, 616-843-8671
5,300 acres featuring a canoe pathway passing reedy swamps and ponds filled with wildlife and flowers. Eleven marked hiking trails and sixteen miles of cross-country ski trails. Three campgrounds in the park offer 400 campsites.

Mackinac Island, 800-833-7711
1,800 acres of pine forest hiking and biking—*no cars allowed*. Mission Point resorts offers two-day Family Adventure Package.

Minnesota
Minnesota Tourism, 800-657-3700

Voyageurs National Park, International Falls, 218-283-9821
Thirty lakes provide fishing, canoeing, powerboating, and swim-

ming. Facilities include visitor centers, naturalist-guided boat and hiking tours, canoe and boat rentals, and outfitting services. Winter camping and hundreds of miles of cross-country skiing, snow-shoeing, and snowmobiling trails. Ice fishing is popular in winter. The park has 130 primitive boat-in campsites. Public and private campgrounds accessible by car are near the park. There are thirty-two miles of maintained hiking trails, accessible only by watercraft.

Forestville State Park/Mystery Cave, Wykoff, 507-352-5111
2,400-acre park featuring a restored 1899 "Old West" town and the state's largest cave. There are 153 campsites to choose from.

Mississippi

Jackson Visitors Information, 800-354-7695

Holly Springs National Forest, Holly Springs, 601-252-2633
147,000 acres of forest and forty lakes for anglers, swimmers, campers, and picnickers. Puskus Lake, covering ninety-six acres, offers remote, primitive camping. A mile-long walking trail leads through a mixed pine forest.

Clarkco State Park, Quitman, 601-776-6651
815-acre park featuring fishing and boating on the Clarkco Lake.

Missouri

Missouri Travel Information, 800-877-1234

Mark Twain National Forest, Rolla, 314-364-4621
1.5 million acres of valleys and foothills in the Ozark Mountains. Forty campgrounds and picnic sites, 350 miles of streams, lakes ranging from ten to 440 acres, and seven wilderness areas totaling more than 63,000 acres. Hundreds of miles of trails for hiking, biking, and horseback riding, and 125 miles of trails for off-road vehicles.

Lake of the Ozarks State Park, Kaiser, 314-348-2694
Wooded hillsides, savannahs, stalactite-filled caverns, a lake and

miles of shoreline. Ten multi-use trails and an aquatic trail marked by buoys. Large campground features riding stables, boat launches, and a swimming beach.

Montana

Montana Travel Information, 800-VISIT-MT

Yellowstone National Park
Information: 307-344-7381
Reservations: 307-344-7311
　　A variety of cabins offer access to Yellowstone's famous canyon, geysers, and hot springs. See detailed listing under Idaho.

Lewis and Clark National Forest, Great Falls, 406-791-7700
　　Forest and mountain terrain includes twenty-four campgrounds and picnic areas, five cabins, an extensive trail system for foot and motorized travel, two alpine ski areas, and miles of marked and groomed snowmobile and cross-country skiing trails. Motorboating, fishing, and raft trips are popular.

Flathead Lake State Park, Kalispell, 406-752-5501
　　2,606 acres including Wild Horse Island, a 2,163-acre island wilderness with strictly controlled boat access and day hikes only. Other areas of the park offer 128 campsites and canoeing.

Nebraska

Nebraska Tourist Information, 800-228-4307

Fort Robinson State Park, Crawford, 308-665-2900
　　An historical/educational park, it also offers hiking, camping, horseback riding, and off-road vehicle trails. The park's 22,000 acres contain wild open grasslands and buttes. There are trails throughout, one of which passes through a bison pasture. Visitors can stay in historic officers' quarters or camp at modern facilities or year-round primitive sites.

Rock Creek Station Historic Park, Fairbury, 402-729-5777
    400-acre park offers hiking and historic glimpse of the Pony Express and Oregon Trails. Park is adjacent to Rock Glen State Wildlife management Area, offering 700 acres of hiking and camping sites.

Nevada
Nevada Tourist Information, 800-NEVADA-1

Lake Tahoe Nevada State Park, Incline Village, 702-831-0494
    13,400-acre park features the famed Flume Trail, a mountain-bike track whose 2,000-foot drop follows the path of the old log flume from the mountains to the lake. Twenty-three miles of shore-front paths for cyclists and hikers. Tahoe and several other lakes provide fishing, swimming, and boating. Also backcountry biking, backpacking, horseback expeditions, and cross-country skiing in season.

Great Basin National Park, Baker, 702-234-7331
    Four developed campgrounds and two primitive camping areas. Cave exploration and backcountry hiking to alpine lakes, a bristle-cone pine grove, a glacier, streams, and meadows. Trails range in difficulty from easy to arduous. Much of the park's backcountry is at elevations of 9,000 feet and above. Hiking, fishing, cross-country skiing, and mountain biking are available.

New Hampshire
New Hampshire Tourism, 800-FUN-IN-NH
Ski Resorts, 800-88-SKI-NH

White Mountain National Forest, Laconia, 603-466-2713
    773,000-acre forest features outstanding hiking, including 1,200 miles of trails, 100,000 acres of wilderness areas, camping, swimming, fishing, hunting, mountain biking, downhill and cross-country skiing, and snowshoeing.

Franconia Notch State Park, Franconia, 603-823-5563
    6,500-acre park, set amidst towering mountain ranges, features

the 80-passenger aerial tram railway, the Flume rock chasm, Echo, Profile, and Lonesome lakes, and the basin glacial pothole. Hiking, fishing, and camping available.

New Jersey
New Jersey Tourism 800-537-7397

Batsto Historic Village and Wharton State Forest, Hammonton, 609-561-3262

110,000 acres including historic Batsto Village, a restored agricultural community from the 1880s. Hiking, canoeing, and nine campsites.

Pinelands National Reserve, New Lisbon, 609-894-9342

One million acres of marshes, bogs, ponds, and dwarf pines. The 18,000-acre Bass River State Forest, in Burlington County in the heart of the Pinelands, features sixty-seven-acre Lake Absegami and facilities for boating, canoeing, swimming, camping, picnicking, hiking, horseback riding, hunting, and fishing.

New Mexico
New Mexico Department of Tourism, 800-545-2070

Santa Fe National Forest, Santa Fe, 505-988-6940

1.567 million acres with elevations ranging from 5,300 feet in White Rock Canyon along the Rio Grande to 13,101 feet at the summit of Truchas Peak. 1,002 miles of trails, twenty-three campgrounds, thirteen picnic areas, and several scenic routes. Opportunities abound for hiking, horseback riding, mountain biking, and exploring by four-wheel-drive vehicle.

Oliver Lee Memorial State Park in Alamogordo, 505-437-8284

Forty-four campsites in a desert setting offering hiking trails and an oasis with a sixty-foot waterfall.

New York
New York Tourism 800-225-5697

Fire Island National Seashore, Patchogue, 516-289-4810
Thirty-two miles along Long Island's south shore; most visitors arrive by ferry. The seashore has fishing, clamming, swimming, walking, and guided nature walks.

Watkins Glen State Park, Watkins Glen, 607-535-4511
Located in the Finger Lakes region, features a two-mile trough created by glaciers, creating nineteen waterfalls and 300-foot shale and sandstone cliffs. 300 campsites, hiking trails, active recreation programs, and two prime fishing lakes.

North Carolina

North Carolina Travel and Tourism, 800-847-4862 or 800-VISIT NC

Great Smoky Mountains National Park, 800-365-2267
Great Smoky Mountains National Park, Cherokee, 615-436-1200 or 800-365-2267
The largest wilderness sanctuary in the East offers nature walks, horse and foot trails, camping, fishing, and wildlife observation. A permit is required for wilderness backpacking. Ten campgrounds and a lodge (accessible only by hiking).

Hanging Rock State Park, Danbury, 910-593-8480
Sheer cliffs, rushing waterfalls, and quiet forests on 6,000 acres ribboned with eighteen miles of wooded hiking trails. A mountain lake supports boating, swimming, and fishing, with plentiful stocks of bass and bream. The north section of the park provides access to the Dan River, a popular canoe and kayak trail.

North Dakota

North Dakota Tourism Department, 800-HELLO-ND

Theodore Roosevelt National Park, Medora, 701-623-4466
A fourteen-mile scenic drive, nature trails, and backcountry trails lead to dry water gulches and petrified forest of this wild and remote region. Roosevelt's former ranch is here, along with boat trips, self-guided trails, and backcountry camping.

Fort Abraham Lincoln State Park, Mandan

1,000 acres recreating life in 1873, with ninety campsites available.

Ohio
Ohio Tourism Information, 800-BUCKEYE

Wayne National Forest, Athens, 614-592-6644

"Ohio's Outback" has the state's highest hills, steepest ravines, and most beautiful waterfalls. Camping, hiking trails, horseback riding, off-road vehicles, plus places to launch a boat, canoe, fish, swim, and picnic. Plus the Covered Bridge Scenic Byway.

Shawnee State Park, Portsmouth, 614-858-6652

1,100 acres in the Appalachian foothills plus a marina on the Ohio River, offers hiking, biking, and backcountry camping. 172 developed campsites, cabins, and a lodge. Boating and canoeing are popular and there is fishing in the river and on two lakes.

Malabar Farms State Park, Lucas, 419-892-2784

914-acre working farm lets your family experience farm life as it was in the 1940s. Accommodations available in the old farmhouse.

Oklahoma
Oklahoma Tourism and Recreation, 800-652-6552

Chickasaw National Recreation Area, Sulphur, 405-622-3165

10,000-acre recreation area includes mineral springs, streams, lakes, camping, and eighteen miles of hiking trails. The Lake of the Arbuckles, the park's dominant feature, and Travertine and Rock creeks attract swimmers and canoeists.

Beavers Bend and Hochatown State Parks, Broken Bow, 405-494-6452

3,482 mountainous acres of land and 14,240 lake acres. There are cabins, a nature center, amphitheater, twenty-six-mile hiking trail, biking trails, backcountry camping, and water sports. Lakeside cabins and more than 300 campsites.

Oregon

Oregon Tourism Division, 800-547-7842

Crater Lake National Park, Crater Lake, 541-594-2511

The second deepest lake in North America, with slopes in the Cascade Range rising to 8,000 feet. Ninety miles of strenuous hiking trails, mountain biking, and two developed campgrounds, plus wilderness backpacking. In winter, backcountry ski camping and snowshoe camping.

Cape Lookout State Park, Tillamook, 800-452-5687

2,000-acre park offers views of seals and gray whales. Traditional campsites and "yurts" available. A yurt is a circular tent with wooden floors, electricity, a space heater, a bunk bed, and a foldout couch. Available for camping in any of eight state parks along the coast. Only $25.00 per night.

Pennsylvania

Tourism, 800-847-4872

Delaware Water Gap National Recreation Area, Bushkill, 717-588-2435

Historic sites include turn-of-the-century Millbrook Village, the 1890s Slateford Farm, and the Van Campen Inn. One campground.

Ohiopyle State Park, Ohiopyle, 412-329-8591

188,000 acres of rugged wilderness in Laurel Mountain's fourteen-mile-long Youghiogheny River Gorge provides some of the best white-water rafting and kayaking in the East. Bicyclists and hikers share twenty-eight miles of rails-to-trails paths along streambeds and past waterfalls.

Rhode Island

Rhode Island Tourism, 800-556-2484

Arcadia Management Area, Richmond, 401-277-1157

14,000-acre forest offers fifty miles of multiple-use trails. For fishing and canoeing, there are streams and three ponds. Stocked and native trout share the waters with some bass. Cross-country skiing when conditions permit.

East Beach State Park, Charlestown, 401-322-0450
3.5-mile beach park requires four-wheel drive to access campsites.

South Carolina
South Carolina Travel Guide, 800-346-3634

Sumter National Forest, Columbia, 803-561-4000
600,000 acres from the foothills of the Blue Ridge Mountains to the Atlantic Ocean. The Chattooga Wild and Scenic River is one of the nation's most popular and scenic waterways. Five wilderness areas offering a range of nature-oriented activities.

Table Rock State Park in Pickens, 803-878-9813
3,100 acres featuring hiking trails among mountains, waterfalls, and two lakes. Fourteen cabins with fireplaces and a seventy-five-site campground with full amenities.

South Dakota
South Dakota Tourism, 800-S-DAKOTA

Badlands National Park, Interior, 605-433-5361
Prime attractions are fossils and unusual rock formations. 64,000 acres for hiking, backpacking, horseback riding, and camping; and a lodge. No formal trails—just those created by bison herds, who still roam. Bicycling on designated roads, including the twenty-three-mile Sage Creek Loop, which offers splendid views and wildlife viewing.

Newton Hills State Park, Canton, 605-987-2263
Tranquil, rolling woodlands feature wildlife, including deer, small mammals, and wild turkeys. Four miles of trails for hikers,

mountain bikers, and equestrians. 123 campsites and two cabins. Cross-country skiing and snowshoeing in season.

Tennessee

Great Smoky Mountains National Park, 615-436-1200
In the Appalachian Highlands, it contains the largest wilderness sanctuary in the East. Nature walks, horse and foot trails, camping, wilderness backpacking, fishing, and wildlife observation. Visitors can hike to cabins at LeConte Lodge (615-429-5704).

Reelfoot Lake State Resort Park, Tiptonville
25,000-acre park, with nature trails and pontoon boat tours. 114 campsites and a nearby inn.

Texas

Texas Visitors Information, 800-88-88-TEX

Guadalupe Mountains National Park, Salt Flat, 915-828-3251
86,000 acres contains Texas' highest peak and eighty miles of trails through deserts, canyons, and highlands. Two campgrounds and ten backcountry campsites.

Brazos Bend State Park, Needville, 409-553-5101
More than seventy campsites available in this nearly 5,000-acre park, home to armadillos, rabbits, and reptiles.

Utah

Utah Tourism 800-233-8824

Zion National Park, Springdale, 801-772-3256
A desert swamp, a petrified forest, springs and waterfalls, with wildlife including roadrunners, golden eagles, mule deer, lizards, and Gambel's quail. Guided horseback trips, technical climbing, backpacking, and biking. A lodge and restaurant available.

Wasatch Mountain State Park, Midway, 801-654-1791
A golf course, plus 139 campsites, picnicking, hiking, and horse-

back riding. Snowmobiling and cross-country skiing are popular winter activities.

Dead Horse Point State Park, Moab, 801-259-2614
Campsites throughout this 5,000-acre park with views of the Colorado River Canyon.

Vermont

Vermont Tourism, 800-VERMONT

Green Mountain National Forest, Rutland, 802-773-0300
100 miles includes 353,000 acres featuring back roads that lace the forest, providing access for foliage viewers, blueberry pickers, hikers, campers, anglers, and hunters.

Ascutney State Park, Windsor, 802-674-2060
3,144 feet high and surrounded by 2,000 acres of parkland. Mount Ascutney has a network of scenic, interconnecting hiking trails. Campgrounds and lean-tos along trails at the foot of the mountain. Hang gliding is popular.

Virginia

Virginia Tourism, 800-VISIT-VA

Colonial Williamsburg, 800-HISTORY

Shenandoah National Park, 703-999-2243 or 800-999-4714
A 195,000-acre hiker's paradise. Trails lead to waterfalls, clear rushing streams, old homesites, and scenic vistas off Skyline Drive. Wildflowers, birds, and white-tailed deer are abundant. 500 miles of trails including part of the Appalachian Trail. 200-site campground and beautiful cabin accommodations in the Blue Ridge Mountains.

Grayson Highlands State Park, Mouth of Wilson, 540-579-7092
5,000 acres in the Appalachian Mountains offering mountain biking, hiking, cross-country skiing, horseback riding, and fishing amidst "semi-wild" ponies. The park is adjacent to 5,729-foot Mount

Rogers, the highest peak in Virginia.

Grayson Highlands State Park, Mouth of Wilson, 703-579-7092
Hiking, horseback riding, camping amidst "semi-wild" ponies.

Washington

Olympic National Park, Port Angeles, 360-452-0330
Diverse terrain includes a fog-shrouded coast, booming surf, wave-sculpted beaches, alpine lakes, lush meadows, glaciers, and temperate rain forest. Fifty-seven miles of coastline, sixty glaciers, and record-size trees. Day hikes, backpacking, soaking in hot springs, climbing Mount Olympus. Downhill and cross-country skiing and snowshoeing in season.

Mount Rainier National Park, Ashford, 360-569-2275
378 square miles of moist rain forests and giant ancient forests, subalpine meadows, glaciers, and rocky outcrops. Mount Rainier is nearly 14,411 feet high (to climb, you have to register). 240 miles of trails. Guided snowshoe walks, horseback riding, and animal trekking available. Five campgrounds, three visitor centers, two inns, and a museum.

Fort Canby State Park, Ilwaco, 360-642-3078
This park stands where the Columbia River meets the Pacific Ocean. Families can explore two of the oldest lighthouses on the West Coast.

Island Institute on Spieden Island, 206-463-6722
Get close to orca whales, otters, sea lions, seals, and porpoises, while enjoying snorkeling, hiking, kayaking, and charter boat rides.

West Virginia

West Virginia Travel Information, 800-CALL-WVA

Appalachian National Scenic Trail, Harper's Ferry, 304-535-6331
2,147-mile Appalachian Trail stretches from Mount Katahdin in central Maine to Springer Mountain in north Georgia. The trail has

more than 500 access points and offers short- or long-term hiking, wildlife and bird-watching, and other backcountry pursuits. It crosses fourteen states, eight national forests, six national parks and sixty state parks and game preserves. Three-sided shelters are provided every ten to twelve miles along the trail and other lodging is available nearby. Camping between shelters is not permitted along most trail areas. Of the 1,200 people who attempt to hike the entire trail each year, only 200 succeed.

Watoga State Park, Charleston, 304-799-4087
Forested park includes an eleven-acre lake, hiking and equestrian trails, and campground. Fishing is excellent in the lake. The park contains an arboretum, the Civilian Conservation Corps Memorial Museum, a variety of cabins and campgrounds, and extensive summer events. Cross-country skiing in season.

Wisconsin
Wisconsin Tourism, 800-22-DELLS or 800-432-TRIP

Apostle Islands National Lakeshore, Bayfield, 715-779-3397
Twenty-two islands in Lake Superior offer hiking, backpacking, fishing, camping, picnicking, boating, sailing, sea kayaking, and scuba diving. Ranger-led island tours, lighthouse tours, bird walks, bog and beach walks, and tours of the historic fish camp on Manitou Island are available. Cross-country skiing, snowshoeing, ice fishing, and winter camping in season.

Willow River State Park, Hudson, 715-386-5931
2,800 acres featuring two lakes, three waterfalls, trout streams, and a pond. Eighty campsites.

Wyoming
Wyoming Division of Tourism, 800-CALL-WYO

Grand Teton National Park, Moose, 307-739-3300
Towering more than a mile above Jackson Hole and the Snake River, the Grand Teton rises 13,770 feet. A mecca for mountain

climbers, hikers, cyclists, skiers, paddlers, and boaters. Three visitor centers and five campgrounds.

Yellowstone National Park
Information: 307-344-7381
Reservations: 307-344-7311
See listing under Idaho.

Teton Country Covered Wagon Adventure
American Wilderness Experience
800-444-0099
Experience the nostalgia of the Old West, with some of the comforts of today, including rubber tires, cushioned seats, and three-course dinners.

Chapter 18

READING RESOURCES

Books

Fun

Brandenburger, Caroline. *The Traveler's Handbook*. Globe Pequot.

Butler, Arlene. *Traveling With Children and Enjoying It*. Globe Pequot.

Clarkson, Clay and Sally. *The Wholehearted Child*. Whole Heart Press.

Frommer, Arthur. *New World of Travel*. Prentice-Hall.

Jordon, Dorothy. *Great Vacations With Your Kids*. E. P. Dutton.

Kaye, Evelyn. *Family Travel*. Blue Penguin Publications.

Lansky, Vicki. *Trouble-Free Travel With Children*. The Book Peddlers.

McMenamin, Paul. *The Ultimate Adventure Sourcebook*. Turner Publishing.

Fitness

Barkin, Roger. *The Father's Guide: Raising a Healthy Child*. Fulcrum.

Bennett, Jeff. *The Complete Whitewater Rafter*. Ragged Mountain Press.

Caldwell, John. *The Cross-Country Ski Book*. Viking/Penguin.

Davis, Don, and Dave Carter. *Mountain Biking*. Human Kinetics.

Fletcher, Colin. *The Complete Walker III*. Knopf.

Glover, Bob. *The Runner's Handbook*. Penguin Books.

Gullion, Laurie. *Canoeing*. Human Kinetics.

Iknoian, Therese. *Fitness Walking*. Human Kinetics.

Manning, Harvey. *Backpacking: One Step at a Time*. Vintage Books.

Oliver, Peter. *Bicycling: Touring and Mountain Bike Basics*. W. W. Norton.

Seaborg, Eric, and Ellen Dudley. *Hiking and Backpacking*. Human Kinetics.

Sheehan, George. *Personal Best*. Rodale Press.

Stewart, Gordon. *Active Living*. Human Kinetics.

Food

Appleton, Nancy. *Lick the Sugar Habit*. Avery Publishing.

Diamond, Harvey and Marilyn. *Fit for Life*. Warner Books.

Diamond, Harvey and Marilyn. *Living Health*. Warner Books.

Dufty, William. *Sugar Blues*. Warner Books.

Frahm, David and Anne. *Healthy Habits*. Pinon Press.

McDougall, John. *The McDougall Plan*. New Century Publishers.

Rucker, Chris, and Jan Hoffman. *The Seventh-Day Diet*. Random House.

Smith, Pamela. *Eat Well, Live Well*. Creation House.

Smith, Pamela. *Food for Life*. Creation House.

Townsley, Cheryl. *Food Smart*. Pinon Press.

Weissman, Joseph. *Choose to Live*. Penguin Books.

Magazines

Adventure Road, 30400 Van Dyke Ave., Warren, MI 48093

American Angler, Northland Press, P.O. Box 280, Rte. 16, Intervale, NH 03845-0280, Editorial: 603-356-9425

American Bicyclist, 400 Skokie Blvd. #395, Northbrook, IL 60062

American Hiker, P.O. Box 20160, Washington, DC 20041

American Whitewater Affil. Mag., P.O. Box 85, Phoenicia, NY 12464

Aquatics, 6255 Barfield Rd., Atlanta, GA 30328-4318, Editorial: 404-256-9800

Audubon, 950 Third Ave., New York, NY 10022-2705

Backpacker, 33 E. Minor St., Emmaus, PA 18098, 800-666-3434

Bicycling Magazine, 33 East Minor St., Emmaus, PA 18098

Bike, 33046 Calle Aviador, P.O. Box 1028, San Juan Capistrano, CA 92675, 800-289-0636

Bird Watcher's Digest, Box 110, Marietta, OH 45750

Boating, 1633 Broadway, 43rd floor, New York, NY 10019

Camping & RV Magazine, P.O. Box 458, Washburn, WI 54891

Camping Today, 126 Hermitage Rd., Butler, PA 16001

Canoe & Kayak Magazine, 10526 NE 68th, P.O. Box 3146, Kirkland, WA 98083, 800-678-5432

Climbing Magazine, P.O. Box 339, 502 Main St., Carbondale, CO 81623

Complete Traveler, 3207 Fillmore St., San Francisco, CA 94123

Conde Nast Traveler, 360 Madison Ave., New York, NY 10017, 800-777-0700

Cross-Country Skier, 1823 Fremont Ave. So., Minneapolis, MN 55403

Cycle World, 853 West 17th, Costa Mesa, CA 92627

Great Expeditions, P.O. Box 18036, Raleigh, NC 27619

National Geographic Traveler, 1145 17th St. NW, Washington, D.C. 20036, 800-638-4077

Outdoor America, 1401 Wilson Blvd. Level B, Arlington, VA 22209

Outdoor Life, 2 Park Ave., New York, NY 10016-5695

Outside Magazine, 400 Market St., Santa Fe, NM 87501, 800-678-1131

Paddler Magazine, P.O. Box 775450, 810 Lincoln Ave., Steamboat Springs, CO 80477, Editorial: 303-879-1450

Sailing World, 5 John Clark Rd., Newport, RI 02840-0992

Sea Kayaker, 6327 Seaview Ave. NW, Seattle, WA 98107

Ski Magazine, Two Park Ave., New York, NY 10016-5601

Skiing, 2 Park Ave., New York, NY 10016

Snow Country, 5520 Trumbull Ave. #395, Trumball, CT 06611-0395

Surfer, 33046 Calle Aviador, San Juan Capistrano, CA 92675, 800-289-0636

Touring America, P.O. Box 6050, Mission Viejo, CA 92690

Travel America, 990 Grove St., Evanston, IL 60201-4370

Travel Holiday, 19 West 22nd St., New York, NY 10010

Travel & Leisure, 1120 Ave. of the Americas, New York, NY 10036, 800-888-8728 Ext. 242

Travelin', P.O. Box 23005, Eugene, OR 97402-9932, 800-345-9828

Vacations, 1502 Augusta Dr. #415, Houston, TX 77057-2484

Weekends Magazine, 481 Bronson Rd., Southport, CT 06490

WindSurfing Magazine, 330 W. Canton Ave., Winter Park, FL 32789